PRACTICAL LAW

Paul C. Cline, J.D., Ph.D., Professor of Political Science,
James Madison University

P. Tony Graham, Ed.D., Associate Professor of Education,
James Madison University

Jesse S. Liles, Ed.D., Associate Professor of Education,
James Madison University

Legal Consultant
Robert Veit Sherwin, Attorney

Holt, Rinehart and Winston, Publishers
New York, Toronto, London, Sydney

Photo credits are on page 150.

Printed in the United States of America
ISBN: 0-03-044146-3

9012 071 9876543

Introduction

Chapter 1
THE LAW, THE POLICE, AND THE COURTS

Chapter 2
CIVIL LAW: Settling Disputes Between Persons

Chapter 3
THE BILL OF RIGHTS

Chapter 4
CRIMINAL LAW AND YOUR RIGHTS

Chapter 5
CORRECTIONS

ONE STEP BEYOND

FOCUS ON CAREERS

CHARTS

INTRODUCTION

This is a book on practical law. Its emphasis is on two things: (1) understanding the basic concepts of the law and (2) applying these concepts to real-life situations. The aim of the book is to acquaint you with the processes of the law and the ways in which the law affects individuals like yourself.

However, this book is not meant to be a substitute for the advice and counsel of an attorney. One reason for this is that legal rules vary from state to state. Another is that only a lawyer, trained in interpreting and applying the law, can relate the facts of a situation to the legal rules that apply to these facts.

In attempting to make this book as practical and helpful as possible, we have relied on our background and our experiences in education and in the law. One author is trained in the law, while the others have long experience in education and classroom teaching. In addition to this, we have conducted many institutes in law-related subjects and have led in-school workshops to train teachers in practical law. Our experiences with classroom teachers have been especially valuable and have been drawn upon in preparing this book.

After reviewing the material in the textbook, the teacher may want to ask a local attorney to participate in the class in some way. For example, he or she may be helpful in leading certain discussions, or in playing the role of judge called for in some activities. While the teacher has the ultimate responsibility for community-based, law-related education, we feel that such education can be enriched by the participation of attorneys on various levels—planning, teaching, and follow-up. From our long association with attorneys, we have found that these professionals are both willing and eager to help in the classroom teaching of law.

We wish to express our thanks to the teachers and members of the bar who have participated in the James Madison Institutes on Law-Related Education which we have conducted.

THE LAW, THE POLICE, AND THE COURTS

Can you imagine a society without rules? In such a community who would say how one person should act with respect to other members of the community? Would people feel compelled to obey guidelines?

Our society has many rules to guide our actions. These rules, or laws, are made by the legislature, by long-standing customs, defined and accepted by judges, and by a variety of other ways. They provide a basis for determining what is and what is not acceptable behavior in society.

To carry out the laws we have a large and complex system of justice. It is used to find out whether a particular kind of behavior violates the laws of society. If the behavior is found to be legally wrong, the system of justice decides what **penalties** *must be paid to society and to individuals who have been harmed by the behavior.*

Police officers are among the most numerous and most visible officials of our system of justice. Today, the duties of the police are varied and difficult. They must be well-informed about the law, must often know how to use complicated equipment such as computers, and must even have a working knowledge of various life-saving techniques. Because crime is growing across the nation, greater emphasis is being placed on the training of police officers than ever before.

The courts are another important part of our system of justice. Although they are not as visible as the police, they play a vital role in keeping order in society. They see that the law is administered fairly and quickly. They have the power to decide whether or not a law has been broken and what penalty must be paid. They decide whether a law passed by the legislature is constitutional, that is, whether it agrees with the Constitution of the United States. The Constitution is the supreme law of our society. The court system is large, containing many courts from the local traffic court to the Supreme Court of the United States. A judge—elected or appointed—presides over each court.

To explain what our legal system is, where it came from, and what services it performs in the community.

To describe the difference between criminal law and civil law.

To describe duties performed by the police department in the community.

To list the steps in a typical investigation of a murder case.

To explain how the court system is organized and what the difference is between appellate courts and trial courts.

To describe the qualifications and tasks of judges.

CHAPTER PREVIEW

1. OUR LEGAL SYSTEM
2. THE POLICE
3. THE COURTS

---

1. OUR LEGAL SYSTEM

What Law Is The word law refers to the rules that state how members of a community should act. In other words, law governs our behavior as parts of a whole called a community. The community may be a nation, a state, or a locality. The word law can refer to a whole system of rules, or to one rule.

When a person or group is found to have broken the law, a **penalty** must be paid. The kind of penalty is determined by the community. For example, someone may have to pay a large sum of money, spend time in jail, or perform some kind of public service. It is believed that members of the community will be more likely to obey the law if they know that they will be penalized for breaking it.

The part of the community that makes the rules and sets the penalties for breaking them varies from society to society. In a democratic society such as ours, most of the rules are made by the people through their representatives in lawmaking groups such as Congress, state assemblies, and city councils. These lawmaking bodies also set most of the penalties for breaking the rules. The system of justice then has the responsibility of carrying out the law and applying specific penalties to those who fail to follow the community's rules.

It is up to officials in our corrections systems to see to it that lawbreakers pay their penalties in the way set down by the laws of the community.

A **penalty** (PEN-ull-tee) is a punishment imposed for breaking the law.

Laws are made by people through their representatives in sessions such as the one pictured here. How many different roles do you see being carried out?

What Law Does   The law performs a number of services for the community. First, it settles the question of how members of the community are supposed to relate to each other. It also states which actions are proper and which are not. Members of the community can then predict the results of their actions. For example, if your community has a rule that no cars may be parked downtown between 8 A.M. and 4 P.M., people who park downtown during this time know that they will be penalized for doing so. Or, if your community has a $500 fine for people found selling firecrackers, someone who sets up a business selling firecrackers knows that he or she will probably have to pay up to $500 if he or she is caught.

A second job of the law is to keep order in the community by controlling the actions of citizens. This can be very important in times of social change or disaster, when disorder is a real threat to the community. For example, during a widespread electric power failure, a community may be threatened with **looting** or rioting. The law works to maintain order at such times by setting severe penalties for both actions.

Third, the law performs the service of educating the community about right and good actions and beliefs. In doing this, the law assumes a task that has become more and more difficult for the family, the school, and religious organizations to perform as our society has become larger and more complex. By providing special help to elderly citizens, such as discounts on public transportation, medical assistance, and senior citizens' centers, the law shows the community the proper way to treat its older members.

Looting means to take the goods of others by force.

 The roots of our legal system are found in many places. One root is found in the **common law** which began in England in the thirteenth and fourteenth centuries. At that time, the king and his officers established a system of courts all over the country. Before that time, various places had their own local system of justice. Laws and penalties often differed from place to place. With the new system of royal courts, all of England would use the same system of laws and penalties. Thus, the law would be common to all members of the large community known as England.

The main feature of the common law is that it is judge-made law. This means that the law is not written down as a separate body of rules, but that it is found by reading and interpreting the decisions of individual judges in individual cases. Under the common law, a decision about one case is made by looking at similar cases in the past and applying them to the present case. Decisions that are made in the past

A parking ticket is the result of failing to obey the laws of the community.

are known as **precedents.** Courts look to precedents for guidance in deciding how to act on cases that are presented to them now.

Underlying all forms of law in the United States are the principles found in the Constitution. The Constitution determines how the government shall be set up, how it shall work, what rights individual citizens have under the government, and what rights the states have.

An important source of law is **statutes.** These are laws passed by the legislatures of the various levels of government—the Congress, state legislatures, and governing bodies of counties, cities, and localities.

ONE STEP BEYOND—THE COMMON LAW

The United States and most English-speaking nations have obtained much of their tradition in law from England. Before 1178 there was no single body of law that applied throughout England. Local courts decided cases on the basis of the customs of the region. Beginning in 1178, the kings developed a system of royal courts which decided cases throughout the nation. The law that was used in settling disputes was no longer the customs of a local area. Instead, the king's judges applied laws that were **common** to all of England. So, these laws as a group became known as the "common law."

Other written sources of law are treaties, state constitutions, and orders of the executive, such as the state governors and the President.

Not all laws are written, however. **Custom** and **tradition** may be so well established that they have the force of law. If so, they will be followed by the courts in settling cases. For instance, laws having to do with trade and the seas often rest on custom.

Criminal Law vs. Civil Law   Some actions that harm others are thought to be harmful to the entire society as well. These actions are known as **crimes** and are taken care of by the **criminal law.** Other actions are thought to be harmful only to the people actually hurt. These come under the branch of our legal system known as the **civil law.** A person harmed by such actions may sue in court the person who has done the harm. In many cases, a person may be charged with a **crime** by society for harming someone and may also be sued under the civil law by the person harmed.

CASE STUDY

An important difference between criminal and civil law is who brings the case to court. The government—national, state, or local—brings the criminal case to court, and the injured person brings the civil case to court. Most courts handle criminal and civil cases. However, some courts and some judges deal in one or the other branch of law.

Settling Cases   Before a trial in a civil case, judges will encourage settlement between the plaintiff and defendant. Courts encourage settlement because they are terribly overburdened. Huge sums of money are also saved when a case does not go to trial.

CASE STUDY

Courts take only those cases over which they have **jurisdiction.** Jurisdiction is the authority of a court to decide a certain case. Although most courts may hear both criminal and civil cases, the jurisdiction of some courts is limited to one or the other. Federal courts usually handle only cases involving federal laws and state courts deal only with state statutes.

Courts may also handle only those cases that are related to the geographical area in which the court is located. For instance, state

Courts obtain jurisdiction over a defendant by having a law officer serve a summons.

Defendants are those who are being sued in civil court or those who are being tried for crime in a criminal court.

A **summons** (SUMM-unz) is a legal order to appear in court.

courts usually have no authority to hear cases from outside the state boundaries. Sometimes, however, it may be possible to transfer a civil case from a federal court in one area to a federal court in another area. Usually, this is allowed when the parties are from two states and the amount of the suit is more than $10,000.

Courts must ordinarily have jurisdiction over the **defendant.** This is known as **personal jurisdiction.** It is obtained by having a legal officer, such as a sheriff, serve a **summons** by giving the necessary legal papers to the defendant in person. Statutes also make it possible to leave the papers on the door of the defendant's residence, rather than handing them over personally. In certain cases, legal notices in the defendant's local newspaper can also serve the purpose of telling the defendant that a suit has been filed against him or her and that the court is ready to act in the suit.

The Political Role of the Courts   The courts have a political role in society in addition to their **judicial** tasks. The courts interpret the Constitution and laws. By doing this, they can influence the behavior of the nation or state in which the court is located. Courts may, for instance, declare acts of Congress or of the state legislature to be in violation of the federal Constitution. This is called the power of **judicial review.** Courts may also hold actions of government officers to be in violation of national or state constitutions.

This power comes from the judicial power of the courts, and a result is often the changing of some **policy** made by a legislative body. Policy-making is usually considered a political power. However, the courts may share in exercising that power in various ways, such as judicial review.

For example, in declaring unconstitutional laws that kept Black children from attending public schools with other children, the Supreme Court of the United States gave a **judicial opinion.** This means the court interpreted the Constitution of the United States. At the same time, the court was making policy that changed the lives of citizens of this nation.

A **policy** (PAH-luh-see) is a decision as to how to act on something. For example, you may establish the policy of going to bed at 11 P.M. each weekday night.

SECTION checkup

1. What is law?
2. What services does law perform for the community?
3. What are the sources of law?
4. What are **precedents?** Why are they important to the **common law?**
5. In what ways may a court's **jurisdiction** be limited?

Black children were barred from Central High School in Little Rock, Arkansas, despite a Supreme Court ruling to desegregate schools. (1957)

2. THE POLICE

A **constable** (KAHN-stuh-bl) and a **sheriff** (SHARE-iff) are two local law officers.

Early law enforcement in this country copied law enforcement in Great Britain. Thus, there was the office of **constable** in the towns of New England and a county **sheriff** in the sparsely populated South. As the country grew, this pattern was followed. Constables were used in urban areas and county sheriffs in rural areas. However, as the population rose and towns became cities, people found they needed more protection from crime than a constable could provide.

City and County Law Enforcement   In 1844, the first modern city police force was set up in New York City. Because it followed the American tradition of **local autonomy,** it was free from any controls by the next higher level of government. The New York City Police Department soon became the model for police departments in the rest of the country.

Local autonomy (aw-TAHN-uh-mee) means local independence.

Early Western Justice   As the country expanded westward, other types of law enforcement were used. These included citizen groups, called **vigilantes,** and the frontier sheriff. Many exciting stories have been told about frontier sheriffs. Their duties were much the same as sheriffs in the East, but the methods they used to fulfill these duties were often quite different. Also, some western towns elected town marshals to protect them from criminals who came into town to cause trouble.

The New York City Police Department, organized in 1844, became a model for the rest of the country. What changes in police organization have taken place since then?

ONE STEP BEYOND—WILD BILL HICKOK

Wild Bill was one of the most well-known characters of the Old West. His real name was James Butler Hickok, and he was born in Troy Grove, Illinois, on May 27, 1837. He moved from Illinois to Leavenworth, Kansas, in 1855, where he was elected constable of Monticello Township, Johnson County, Kansas. During the Civil War he served as both a scout and spy for the Union forces. Wild Bill was captured several times and was sentenced to be shot, but each time he was able to escape. After the war, in 1866, he was appointed deputy United States Marshal at Fort Riley, Kansas. It was during this period that he also acted as scout for Generals Custer, Sheridan, and Hancock. In 1869, he was appointed marshal of Hays City, Kansas. This was the roughest border town in the West. He was soon able to restore order to the town. However, this was not done without bloodshed. For example, he was attacked by three men at once, and he killed each of them. In 1871 he left Hays City and became marshal of Abilene, Kansas, which had a reputation for lawlessness almost equal to Hays City. By 1872, his fame was well known. He joined Buffalo Bill's Wild West Show and toured the East for a year. Wild Bill's life came to an end in Deadwood, Dakota Territory, on August 2, 1876, when he was murdered by Jack McCall. His fame lives to this day. Wild Bill Hickok's legend and reputation served as a model for the lawmen of his day who never killed except in self-defense or in the line of duty.

"Wild Bill" Hickok served as Marshal for one of the roughest towns in the Old West.

State Law Agencies   The first state law enforcement agency was started in Texas with the organization of the famous Texas Rangers in 1835. The Rangers were set up to keep law and order in an organized fashion in all areas of the Lone Star State. Both Massachusetts and Connecticut also had state police systems before 1900. After this time, other states gradually began developing some type of state police system. By 1939, twenty-four states had a state police system. Today, all the states have a state police agency although all are not called by the same name. For example, the state police in Arizona are called the Arizona Rangers and those in New Mexico are called the New Mexico Police. Many states also have responsibility for investigating crimes. North Carolina, for example, has a state bureau of investigation.

Federal Law Agencies   The Judiciary Act of 1789 created the post of United States Marshal. This was the first law enforcement officer in the federal government. In an effort to prevent smuggling along the seacoast, the Revenue Cutter Service was also established in 1789.

In 1903, the Secret Service acquired the responsibility of protecting the lives of United States presidents.

During the Civil War, **counterfeiting** of Union **currency** became a problem. As a result, in 1865, the Congress created the Secret Service to help restore the confidence of the people in the Union currency by enforcing counterfeiting laws. The Secret Service was to operate under the Treasury Department. In 1903 the role of the Secret Service was expanded to include protecting the life of the President. This action came as a result of the assassination of President William McKinley in 1901. In 1963 John F. Kennedy became the first President to be assassinated while under the protection of the Secret Service.

The forerunner of the Federal Bureau of Investigation was organized in 1880. The FBI itself was a product of a reorganization of the first agency in 1924. In that year, J. Edgar Hoover became the FBI's first director. He served in this post until his death in 1972. The Federal Bureau of Investigation is probably the best known of all federal law enforcement agencies.

In addition to the federal agencies already mentioned, many other agencies also have the responsibility of protecting the American general public. These include the Drug Enforcement Administration, the Internal Revenue Service, the United States Marshals, and the Border Patrol.

Law Enforcement Today   Today, there are more than 500,000 full-time law enforcement officers serving more than 40,000 separate, **autonomous** police agencies on the local, state, and federal levels. Being **autonomous** means that each agency has the responsibility for law enforcement in its locality and that it operates independently of any other law enforcement agency. The advantage of autonomy is that it prevents police from using their power to seize control of the government. It also enables locally recruited and controlled police agencies to adjust their policies and operations to the widely varying needs of our country. However, there are disadvantages to autonomy as well. These include competition rather than cooperation, lack of standard procedures in law enforcement throughout the country, local political interference with the police, and serious differences in the efficiency of police forces.

Today, the police have come under attack by those who feel that they do not attract the kind of people who will be good police officers. It is true that low salaries and a threat of danger have kept many good people away from the police forces. Many localities are now trying to change this in order to have better, more efficient law enforcement officers in the community. They are being helped to do this by a federal agency known as the Law Enforcement Assistance Administration (LEAA). This agency has provided funds to the states to develop programs which will increase the efficiency and effectiveness of law enforcement. This financial support has led to innovative programs at all levels of government. For example, regional training centers and area crime laboratories have been set up by cooperating local governments in order to provide better services for the total area rather than having facilities that do the same job or having no facilities at all.

Police Organization   In rural areas of this country, the top law enforcement officer is the **county sheriff,** who is elected to office. A person who runs for the office need not have any specific qualifications for carrying out the duties normally expected of a sheriff. As a result, law enforcement in the rural areas is controlled by the political powers.

Once the sheriff is elected, he or she organizes a law enforcement body by appointing deputies. A deputy sheriff serves at the pleasure of

In many rural areas, a person desiring the office of county sheriff must campaign for the position in order to win election.

the sheriff. If a new sheriff is elected, especially from an opposing political party, the deputies are often relieved of their duties and other persons who have helped the new sheriff win the election are appointed. In recent years, many sheriffs and deputies have taken courses in law enforcement in an effort to improve the skills needed to do their jobs well. The result has been improvement in rural law enforcement.

The organization of a typical city police department is similar to that of the military. The head of the police department is usually a professional police officer called the chief. In many of the larger cities, there is a civilian department head called the commissioner or director. Here, the chief of police is under the authority of the commissioner. Under the chief, there are numerous supervisory officers arranged in order of rank. These include assistant chiefs, then majors or inspectors, captains, lieutenants, and sergeants. Next come detectives and then patrol officers. Larger cities are usually divided into geographical districts called **precincts.** Since police work is a continuous process, the police force is also organized under a **platoon system,** which allows the force to work on day and night shifts.

The Role of the Police   The role of the police is based largely on the demands and needs of the local community. In recent years, advances in law enforcement have been the result of community reaction to situations such as the riots of the 1960s. As a result of this particular situation, the community realized that there was a need for more equipment, for the establishment of police-community relations units, and for stronger police training and educational requirements.

Since the role of the police is determined by community needs, the police naturally look toward the community for direction. Often this direction has been lacking. Communities have identified most of their needs but have failed to say which they feel are most important. In many cases, when communities do set priorities, such as detecting crime and catching criminals, public service activities such as directing traffic get less attention.

Intensive training makes better law officers. What are other police activities that may require training?

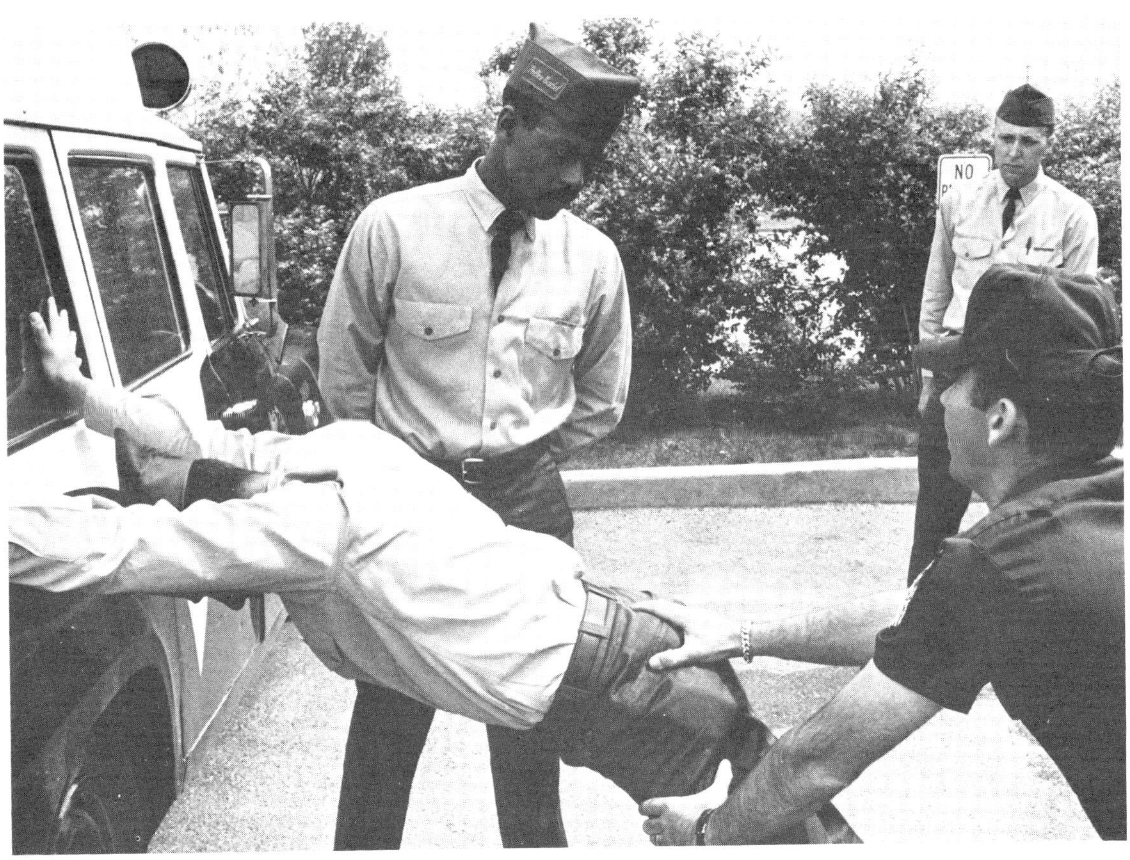

Law officers must often become involved with their communities. Can you think of other ways to meet the needs of the community through involvement?

It is also very difficult to set priorities in a community when each part of the community has different priorities. The end result is that the police may not act in a way that pleases everyone in the community. However, it is still important that they listen to the voice of the community and use common sense and training to meet the needs of the community as closely as possible.

It is generally agreed that the police play three important roles: law enforcement, furnishing services, and keeping the peace. The most common public image of the police officer is that of law enforcer. However, some studies indicate that as few as ten percent of all police calls involve law enforcement. Furnishing services is actually far more common. Doing this involves attending accidents, directing traffic, escorting crowds, helping stranded motorists, or speaking at civic affairs and to school groups. Keeping the peace takes a great deal of time. This involves such duties as breaking up fights, quieting noisy parties, handling family or neighborhood quarrels, and other similar tasks. In most of these incidents, it is often difficult to determine who is to blame. A person involved in a fight cools down and refuses to press charges against the other person. It is in this role that the police exercise the greatest judgment in applying the law. As a result, they are able to add a personal element into the enforcement of the law.

The Use of Force The police officer is legally entitled to use force in the performance of duty when it is reasonable and appropriate. While making an arrest, in self-defense, and in keeping the peace of the community, the police are frequently found in situations that require force to be used if their duty is to be properly performed.

Although a police officer has a legal right to use force, this right seems to make many people suspicious, distrustful, and hostile toward the police. American tradition has always stressed personal freedom, and efforts to regulate behavior have often led to public hostility against the police. However, most people know that the police must have the right to use force in order to protect society in general and individual citizens.

More than anything else police work involves working with people. The police come into constant contact with the worst kind of people and with the best kind of people at their worst. Since no two persons are alike, each encounter the police have with the public must be solved in a different way. The police force is composed of persons with normal backgrounds and experiences. Many of them have little or no professional education in police work. Yet, the public expects them to do their tasks as experts might. In reality, the police are like other people. Sometimes they make mistakes even though they are trying to do their duty as efficiently, effectively, and peacefully as possible.

CASE STUDY

Imagine you were a police officer. While on patrol, you received a radio call to go to a neighborhood where there was a disturbance. When you arrived at the address, you heard a loud crashing sound in the house. Upon knocking and being let in, you found that the wife had been beaten up by her husband, who continued to say insulting things to her and to you. At that point, the wife, realizing what might happen to her husband, began screaming and cursing you as well. What should you do?

A Common Misunderstanding   Many people think that a police officer chasing a fleeing criminal cannot cross the **border** and make an arrest in a neighboring state. In general, this is not true. In over thirty states, a private person may make an arrest if that person knows a crime has been committed and has reasonable ground to believe the person arrested has committed it. When the police officer crosses the state line, he or she automatically becomes a private citizen. As such, he or she may continue pursuing and arrest the suspected criminal.

Criminal Investigation   As far as the general public is concerned, murder is the most fascinating of crimes. Murder is often the subject of television programs, movies, and novels. These dramas depict murder cases for entertainment, and most of them ignore the true hard work done by a police officer in solving such a case. The true investigation of murder is much more routine than glamor.

Developing a case for murder involves putting together information from a variety of sources. Among these is the **medical examiner's report.** This report provides the investigator with the actual cause of death, the number and type of wounds, the probable time of death, and the position of the body after death.

A second source is the **forensic section** of the police department. It takes charge of the scene of the crime as soon as possible after the victim is found. Photographs of the scene and the body are taken immediately and samples of physical evidence such as blood, handwriting, weapons, hair, or fibers are gathered at or near the scene. The information gathered by the forensic section is organized and sent to the detective in charge of the case.

A crucial role in the investigation may be played by the first uniformed police officer to arrive at the scene of the murder. It is the responsibility of this officer to preserve the scene as much as possible. In some cases, the scene might have to be guarded to keep people away. The officer must also detain witnesses to the crime so they can be questioned by detectives. If it is impossible for them to stay, the officer must get their names and addresses and obtain a statement from them. If this is not done immediately, the witnesses often disappear and the chance of solving the crime is reduced.

The responsibility for solving the crime lies with the detective who has been placed in charge of the case. The detective must take all the available evidence and reconstruct the crime as accurately as possible. The detective tries to find out who did what to whom and why. The information obtained from the medical examiner, forensic reports, witnesses, and what is observed at the scene are all used to find out exactly what happened. One of the most important jobs of the detective is locating and interviewing possible witnesses to the crime. Often, this means knocking on hundreds of doors before enough reliable witnesses are found to insure that the person responsible for the crime is caught and convicted.

The first 48 to 72 hours after the crime will usually determine the direction of the investigation. It is very desirable that murder cases be solved as quickly as possible because as time passes, witnesses tend to forget or to color their ideas of what happened, and the criminal has a greater opportunity to flee or hide. Therefore, the homicide detective works quickly and thoroughly to solve the case at the earliest possible moment. For example, a man witnessed a murder in an alley one night. He described the suspect as being tall with red hair. Three days later he called to say that the suspect's hair may have been blonde and curly. The police officers lost valuable time by looking for tall red-headed suspects. If they had questioned this witness a month later he may have come up with still another description or he may not have been able to remember at all.

SECTION CHECKUP

1. What is the name of the first state law enforcement agency to be established? In what year was it organized?
2. What is the purpose of the Law Enforcement Assistance Administration?
3. How is a typical police department organized?
4. How is a murder case investigated? Mention each step in the process.

The Supreme Court, located in Washington, D.C., is the highest court in the United States.

3. COURT ORGANIZATION

The organization of the courts of the United States is only partially established by the constitutions of the United States and the individual states. Usually, the Congress or the state legislatures are allowed to set up special courts as they choose. Also, the courts themselves, particularly the higher courts, frequently have some say in the manner in which the courts are structured.

Appellate Courts   The courts have two types of jurisdiction, according to the type of action that the court is called upon to perform. One type of jurisdiction is called **appellate.** A court with **appellate jurisdiction** hears arguments that claim a lower court made mistakes in handling a particular case. **Original jurisdiction** is the power to hear a case for the first time. Trial courts have almost entirely original jurisdiction, while appellate courts have almost entirely appellate jurisdiction.

The chart on page 19 shows the organization of the federal and state courts. Two levels of appellate courts and three levels of trial courts are shown. The appellate levels are the **courts of last resort** and the **intermediate appellate courts.** Most courts of last resort, so-called because they are at the end of the judicial ladder, are called **supreme courts.** They include the Supreme Court of the United States. Intermediate appellate courts have been formed to assist the courts of last resort by taking part of the workload and settling numerous cases before they get to the top courts. The intermediate appellate courts of the United States system are the courts of appeals.

Trial Courts   Trial courts consist of courts of **general, limited or special,** and **petty jurisdiction.** Courts of general jurisdiction handle major civil and criminal cases. They may also have appellate jurisdiction over cases coming from lower courts. These courts in the federal system are called district courts. There is at least one district court in every state.

The courts of **general jurisdiction** are often called **circuit courts** in the states. The term "circuit" came from the practice of judges going around to a number of counties to try cases, a practice called "riding the circuit." Lawyers, too, would often ride the circuit with the judges. There they represented clients in the various towns in which they stopped. Abraham Lincoln rode the circuit to practice law.

Courts of **limited jurisdiction** handle cases of lesser importance—civil, criminal, or both. Courts of **special jurisdiction** deal with specific matters, such as juvenile cases or suits involving domestic relations. **Domestic relations** are matters involving the family. (Divorce, a family matter, is not handled in special court.)

Numerous lower courts have **petty jurisdiction.** These are the local courts and handle such matters as traffic violations, the breaking of local government ordinances, and minor civil hearings.

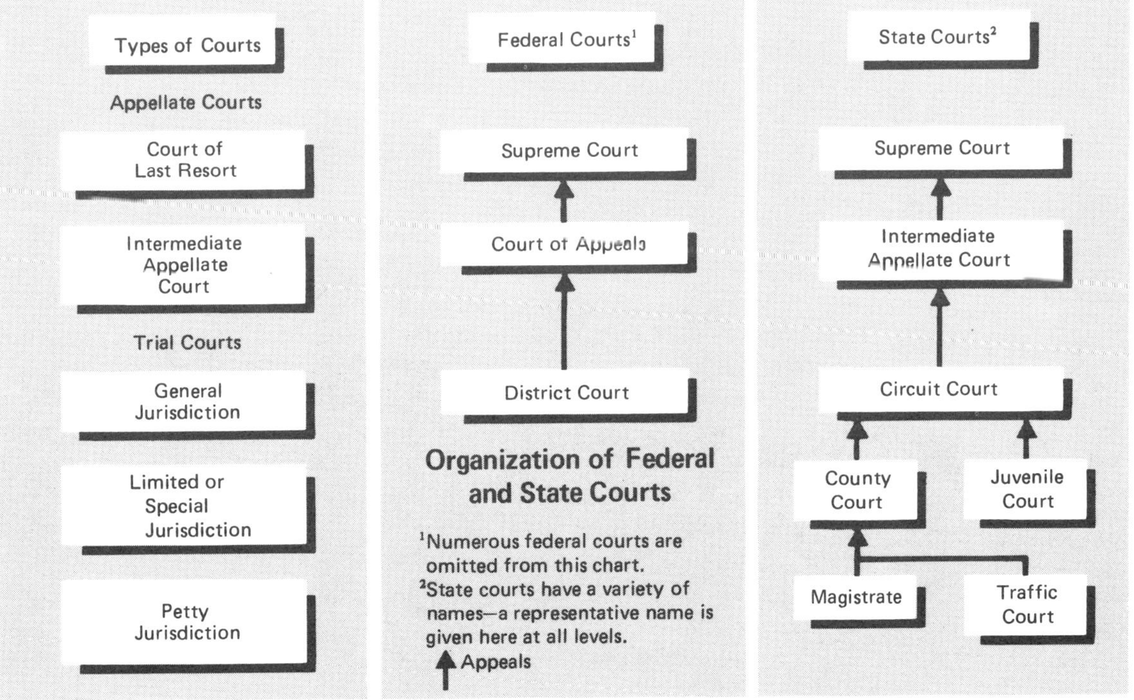

Organization of Federal and State Courts

¹Numerous federal courts are omitted from this chart.
²State courts have a variety of names—a representative name is given here at all levels.

↑ Appeals

Because of the large number of these matters, courts of limited and petty jurisdiction are designed to handle cases quickly. Often, there is no right to a jury trial at this low level. However, if one is convicted at this level, he or she usually has a right to appeal the case to the next higher court. In the courts of general jurisdiction, the person will receive full rights to a jury trial and to have a record made of the case.

The **record** is a written account of the questions of attorneys and the statements of witnesses and the judge. A record is necessary to appeal the case farther up the judicial ladder because appeals judges consider the record of the case in determining whether a lower court made a mistake in giving its decision.

The appeals routes are marked with arrows on the diagram of court organization. Notice that cases are usually not appealed back and forth between the federal and state courts except for an appeal from the state court of last resort to the United States Supreme Court. The highest courts limit the cases they will consider on appeal. As a result, not every case reaches the very top courts. In these cases, the decisions of the lower courts are then the final decision.

Courts are often organized under the leadership of the court of last resort. This court may, under authority given to it by the legislature, set the rules of procedure, require reports, and move judges around throughout the entire judicial system.

CASE STUDY

Judge Putter McGolf has little to do in his court, but Judge Ina C. Daylight, in the adjoining county, cannot catch up with the workload of her court. Can anything be done to equalize these work levels?

Yes, if the chief administrative judges of each court level have their chief judges assign equal workloads to co-judges.

Judges   Judges are at the center of the legal system. They have responsibility for decisions affecting the lives, liberty, and property of the persons appearing before their courts. Judges manage the trials of cases and interpret the law as found in constitutions, statutes, and prior court rulings. If the parties do not desire a trial by jury, the judge may be called upon to interpret not only the law but also the facts of the case.

Some judges believe that they should protect the interests of the public. Others feel that they are to interpret the law without regard to the effects of their interpretation. Most judges will refuse to hear a case in which they are involved in some manner. Even the most precise interpreters of the law are human and may place some of their non-legal attitudes and values into their opinions.

In spite of the fact that a judge usually has his or her own views on a matter, one of the most important characteristics of a good judge is thought to be the ability to give unbiased opinions. After listening to both sides of a controversy, a judge should be able to weigh the arguments and decide the case on the basis of the arguments as they relate to the law.

Other characteristics sought in judges include knowledge of the law, fairness, and compassion. Much of the judge's work involves interpreting legal rules and, for this purpose, knowledge and experience are important. Fairness and compassion may not always be possible in the same decision. For instance, compassion for a defendant may lead to a conclusion that he or she should be dealt with lightly. But this light treatment may not be fair when the position of the person suing is considered. It may also not be fair with regard to past and future defendants in the same position.

A judge must also be able to organize the workload of the court and see that this work gets done. A judge should be able to work with

Legal Secretary

A legal secretary is a secretary with specialized skills. He or she works for a lawyer, a law firm, or a law department within a corporation. Being a legal secretary requires accurate and fast typing and shorthand skills. A knowledge of law vocabulary is also a must. Many times, a legal secretary must enroll in business law courses in order to gain familiarity with special law terms.

Matti DeVico has worked as a legal secretary at the Columbia Broadcasting System for seven years. Before beginning her career, she attended Hunter College for two and one half years. She then went to secretarial school where she prepared for her career as a legal secretary.

In her present position, Ms. DeVico deals with lawyers and business executives. A typical day for her is very busy. She is responsible for answering over one hundred phone calls a day and taking very accurate messages about the calls. She must sort a large volume of mail. She handles many problems in order to keep her boss as undisturbed as possible. When not taking dictation or keeping accurate files, she is busy typing very important reports and legal documents. Her typing must be as free from errors as possible.

Ms. DeVico's job as legal secretary is one which is full of responsibility and pressure which she thoroughly enjoys. Since her beginning as a legal secretary, Ms. DeVico has assumed even more responsibility. The next step for her would be that of a paralegal, who does much of the time consuming research for a lawyer. A legal secretary's job is one of extreme importance and many businesses could not do without one.

people since he or she must interact with jurors, clerks of the court, lawyers, and parties to suits.

In most states judges are elected. However, about half of the states that elect judges do so on a ballot in which the political parties of the candidates are not listed. Federal judges are appointed by the President. The governor and legislature appoint judges in some states. Even where judges are elected by the people, the governor usually fills vacancies which occur between elections. Often lawyers' organizations advise governors as to the merits of lawyers to be considered for appointment.

Judges make decisions that affect the lives, liberty, and property of people in the entire nation.

Judges may be removed by a variety of ways. The legislature may remove unsuitable judges in many states, sometimes after holding a legislative trial to hear the charges against the judges. In a few states, governors may remove unfit judges. A special commission may hear charges and recommend removal to the highest state court, which may take the final action if it wishes.

SECTION CHECKUP

1. What are **appellate** and **original** jurisdiction?
2. Name the two levels of appellate courts.
3. Why is it necessary to make a **record** of a case?
4. What tasks do judges perform?
5. How may judges be removed?

CHAPTER REVIEW

The law performs various functions. For example, it determines which actions are proper, maintains order, and educates people about the right action and belief. The sources of law are varied and include **court cases, statutes,** and **custom.**

In settling cases the courts apply a number of principles. They require that there be a **real controversy** between the parties. It is also necessary for the court to have jurisdiction over the case.

The police serve an important function in our society. We have local, state, and national agencies who operate with autonomy in regard to crimes committed within their jurisdiction. The police force is composed of persons who realize that a certain amount of danger will always be part of the job, and who try to use their concepts of what that community expects as they go about the everyday task of performing their duties.

Courts are organized on **trial** and **appellate** levels, with the appellate courts determining whether trial courts made errors in their handling of cases. Usually, the appellate courts limit the number of cases they will hear from losing parties in lower courts.

Judges have an important role in the judicial system. They are required to be fair and unbiased in their decisions. It is also important that they have a good knowledge of the law and an ability to organize the workload of the courts in order to get the judicial task completed.

QUESTIONS FOR REVIEW

1. What is the **common law?**
2. Describe the political role of the courts.
3. What are the three major roles of the police? Which of these takes most of the time of the police?
4. How are the priorities of the police department determined? Why has this been a problem in recent years?
5. What are the five levels of courts?
6. Name three federal courts in order from the lowest level to the highest.
7. What is the best way to select judges based upon the responsibilities of judges?

1. Sources of Law.   Collect samples of the various sources of law described in the text. A local attorney will be helpful in furnishing some of the sources. Can you find any customs or traditions in your community which have the force of law? A lawyer or business leader in the community may suggest certain business practices in the community which create rights that are upheld in court.

2. Serving Papers.   Contact the local sheriff or other legal officer and ask that person to explain how official court papers are served on individuals so that the court may require their presence at a lawsuit. After learning how this is done in your local area, have members of the class serve papers on other class members personally or in other ways listed in the chapter.

3. You Be the Police Officer.   Read the case study under the section on the police. Write a short description of what you would do if you were that police officer.

4. Courtroom in a Classroom.   Have members of the class visit a local trial courtroom and make simple sketches of the position of the judge's bench, the witness stand, the jury box, and the attorneys' tables. Reproduce the courtroom in the classroom using available desks and other furniture.

Ask a lawyer who has appealed a case to a higher court to describe the courtroom of the appellate court. Reproduce the appellate courtroom in the classroom. The lawyer may also be willing to tell the class about his or her preparation and arguments of the appeal.

YOU AND THE LAW

YOUR LAW LIBRARY

Crime and the Law. Washington, D.C.: Congressional Quarterly, 1971.

Landsman, Stephen, Donald McWherter, and Alan Pfeffer, *What to Do Until the Lawyer Comes: An Invitation to Law.* Garden City, New York: Anchor Press/Doubleday, 1977.

Prassel, Frank R., *The Western Peace Officer.* Norman, Oklahoma: University of Oklahoma Press, 1972.

U.S. News and World Report Books, *What Everyone Needs to Know About the Law.* Washington, D.C.: U.S. News and World Report, Inc., 1973.

CIVIL LAW: Settling Disputes Between Persons

chapter 2

Suppose you have a disagreement with someone in one of the following ways:
1. *Someone says you trespassed on land of his or hers. You say you did not trespass.*
2. *Someone accuses you of breaking an agreement the two of you have made. You deny breaking the agreement.*

*How would you settle these disputes? You might use force, but after the fight, the dispute probably would not be settled. Or, you might sit down with the other person and discuss the problem. This probably wouldn't solve the dispute either, because each of you would see only one point of view—your own. Another way to reach an agreement would be to ask a third person to listen to the facts and to give an opinion. The opinion might be **binding** or **not binding.** This means that both of you might decide to accept the decision (binding), or one or both might decide to reject it (not binding).*

*In our society, serious disputes between people are often settled by the "third person" method. In disputes that need a binding opinion, courts are the "third person" **legal system** that has been set up to settle conflicts between individuals. Other parts of the legal system are the **legislatures,** which make the laws; **attorneys,** who help people to bring their disputes into court; and **agencies** that must see the laws are carried out.*

OBJECTIVES

To be able to describe how the courts settle disputes between people.

To know what **contracts** and **torts** are.

To be able to describe how the law can protect you from **breach of contract** or other types of harm.

To decide whether consumers and the environment are well protected under our present laws.

---

1. HOW THE COURT WORKS TO SETTLE DISPUTES

The **civil law** is the branch of law that settles disagreements between individuals. In criminal law, one party is a person or group accused by the government of breaking the law. In civil law, however, the government is not one of the parties in the case, and neither party is accused of breaking the law.

While the civil law deals with disputes between individuals, it is possible for one or both of the "individuals" to be groups, such as **corporations** or cities. For example, a corporation may be **sued** by another corporation for breaking an agreement. In cases like this, each corporation is not thought of as "many people" but as one "individual" before the law.

Persons or groups who sue in court are called **plaintiffs.** Those being sued are called **defendants.**

Requirements for a Case to Go to Court If a case is to go to court, it must fulfill three requirements:

1. There must be a controversy between parties.
2. The parties must have a right to sue and to be sued.
3. The court must have jurisdiction of the case.

A **controversy** is a real disagreement between the parties. It may not be a fake disagreement in which two friendly individuals try to gain something by staging a court case. Also, one party must have done some actual harm to the other. The individual cannot have just done something that the other one objects to. If a neighbor felt you played your stereo too loud, he or she could take you to court because the sound may have caused real damage, such as interrupting your neighbor's sleep.

A controversy is a dispute that a court can do something about now. It cannot be a **moot** dispute (one that has already been settled).

For example, a female college student applied to law school but was rejected. A male student was admitted to the same school with lower grades on the admission test. The female student sued the law

A **corporation** (kor-por-AY-shun) is a group organized under the law for a special purpose, such as doing business.

To **sue** (SOO) means to take legal action, especially to make a legal claim to something.

school on the grounds that they had discriminated against her. By the time the case reached the highest court, the female student had been admitted to the school and had received her degree. The court said that this was a **moot case.** Can you figure out why?

Also, the court will not hear disputes that have happened so far in the past that a case cannot be based on them. The court will not consider disputes that might occur far in the future either. These are not considered real controversies because the court cannot settle them now.

The party who sues—the plaintiff—must be someone who is harmed in some way. It cannot be someone who is merely interested in the case. For instance, someone who has not had to pay a tax is not allowed to bring a suit into court against those who must collect the tax. Only someone who is required to pay the tax by law can do this. The party who is sued—the defendant—must be the individual who has actually done the harm to the plaintiff. If you are riding in a car that smashes into a parked car, for example, the owner of the parked car cannot sue you. He or she must sue the person who was driving the car in which you were riding.

FOCUS ON CAREERS

Attorneys-at-Law

In order to become a lawyer it is necessary to graduate from a law school program that is three years long. Law school normally comes after four years of college. Another route permitted in a very few states is the "reading" of law. This means serving as an assistant to a lawyer for a certain number of years instead of going to law school.

In most states, it is necessary to pass a **bar** examination to practice law. A bar is a professional association of lawyers, licensed by the state.

A final requirement in order to be "admitted to the bar" to practice law is that a person be of good character. If someone has been convicted of a serious crime, he or she may not be allowed to practice law.

Finally, a court will consider a case only if it has **jurisdiction** of the case. Jurisdiction is the power to consider a certain case. For example, some courts can try only certain kinds of cases. The **juvenile** court can only try cases involving individuals who have not reached a certain age—usually 15 or 16. The jurisdiction of the various courts in our legal system is set by law.

Before the Trial Suppose Andy has been injured by Betty and decides to sue Betty. First, he visits an attorney for advice. The attorney consults law books to see whether Andy has the right to sue Betty for

Three years of law school is the usual requirement for becoming an attorney.

such an injury. He or she might point out to Andy that there are disadvantages to suing Betty. There will be the attorney's fees and other expenses. Andy will certainly have to spend a lot of time seeing the case through to the end, and he might lose.

The attorney may advise Andy to **negotiate** with Betty before deciding to sue. If the negotiations are successful, the case can be settled "out of court." The importance of attorneys in settling controversies like this one is shown by the fact that many, many cases are settled out of court.

If negotiations fail and Andy decides to pursue the case, the attorney will write a **complaint.** In it the attorney will state how the plaintiff—Andy—has been harmed by the defendant—Betty. He will also state that the injury is one which may be **recovered for** by the plaintiff. This means that Andy can receive some kind of payment for having been injured. The complaint also describes the **damages** the plaintiff wants the defendant to provide. Damages are the amount of money for which an injured party sues. They are based upon the kind of harm done to him or her by the other party.

The complaint is served by a law officer or other authorized person on the defendant, and the defendant's attorney has a limited amount of time to file an answer to the complaint. If an answer is not filed, the plaintiff may be able to recover damages without going to trial.

To **negotiate** (nuh-GO-shee-ate) means to discuss something in order to reach a settlement.

A **complaint** (kum PLAYNT) is a statement that says some form of injustice has been done to someone.

To **recover for** (ree-KUV-er) means to get something back by means of a decision in a law court.

1. If Andy is injured by Betty

Andy may drop the matter

or

seek help from an attorney.

2. If Andy seeks help from an attorney

Andy may drop the matter after talking with the attorney

or

have the attorney bring suit against Betty.

3. If Andy has the attorney bring suit against Betty by filing a complaint

Betty may admit she harmed Andy and settle the case,

or

Betty may deny Andy's claim, or deny that Andy has a case, or claim a loss also, or all three at once.

4. If Betty answers Andy's complaint

the case may be settled by the attorneys of Andy and Betty,

or

the case may be settled at a pretrial conference between a judge and the attorneys of Andy and Betty,

or

the case may go to trial before a judge alone or a judge and jury.

5. If the case goes to trial before a judge and jury,

the judge decides the law of the case and the jury decides the facts of the case and gives a verdict.

6. If the losing party disagrees with the verdict,

that party's attorney will make motions to have the verdict set aside. If this is not done, the attorney will appeal the case to a higher court.

7. If the right of appeal is granted by the higher court

both the losing and winning parties' attorneys will present written legal arguments—briefs—and the written record of the case to the higher court. They will also argue the case in person to the higher court.

8. If the higher court upholds one of the parties

the case may be appealed until an even higher court refuses to hear the appeal, or until the highest court is reached.

The defendant's answer may contain various statements. The defendant may claim, for instance, that he or she did not harm the plaintiff. Or, the defendant may state that, if he or she did do harm, the plaintiff has no legal right to sue. The defendant may also challenge the amount of damages listed in the complaint. The complaint may even state that the defendant was injured in some way by the plaintiff and that the plaintiff should pay damages for this injury.

After both parties have received the complaint and the answer, a pretrial conference is held. The judge and the attorneys meet and try to simplify the issues involved in the case. They also try to see if there is any way to settle the dispute before taking it to court.

THE STAGES OF A CIVIL TRIAL

1. Jury members are selected, if a jury is being used.

2. Attorneys make opening statements.

3. Evidence is presented
   —Witnesses appear for the plaintiff and the defendant. Attorneys examine directly the witnesses they have called. Attorneys for the other party cross-examine the witnesses.
   —Real evidence is shown to the court. This includes anything that is offered to prove a point in the trial.

4. Attorneys make closing statements.

5. The judge charges the jury.

6. The jury gives its decision, or verdict, on the case.

7. Attorneys for the plaintiff or the defendant make motions to set aside the verdict because it is incorrect as to law or fact.

8. The judge rules, or makes a decision, on whether to uphold motions to set the verdict aside or to confirm the verdict.

The Trial   The purpose of the trial is to determine the rights of each party in the case. This is done by having each side present **evidence** that supports its point of view or attacks the other party's viewpoint. **Evidence** is everything a court may consider in reaching a decision about the case. The evidence is presented in stages and according to rules set down by the courts or by the law.

The case may be presented to a judge, or to a judge and a jury. The judge decides the **law in the case.** This means he or she determines the right of the parties according to certain standards. These include constitutions, laws, other court decisions, and customs that have the effect of laws.

The jury determines the **facts of the case.** That is, it decides whether or not the plaintiff, the defendant, or the witnesses are speaking the truth. It also decides how much importance to give to evidence presented during the trial. A jury is selected from a group that represents the whole community, not just a part of it. In other words, if there are many elderly people in the community, the jury should have a certain number of elderly members. When no jury is used in a case, the judge decides on both the law and the facts.

The attorneys make opening and closing statements at the trial. But these are not considered evidence in the case. These are attempts by the attorneys to place their clients' cases in the best possible light, or to put the opposition's case in a bad light.

After all the evidence has been presented, the judge gives his **charge** to the jury. The charge is a list of the legal rules that apply to the case. Also included in the charge are the kinds of **verdicts** the jury may choose from in deciding the case. Before the jury can give its verdict, a certain number of the jurors have to agree on it. The number varies from place to place and for different kinds of cases. When the required number of jurors fails to agree on a verdict, the outcome is called a **hung jury.** A new trial is then ordered, or the case is dropped.

A **verdict** (VER-dikt) is a decision made by a jury in a law court about a case that they have been considering.

ON CAREERS

Judges

Judges are usually lawyers, and they must have all the requirements that are necessary to be a lawyer. (See Attorneys-at-Law, page 28.)

Judges are selected in a variety of ways. All federal judges are appointed by the President. Although most state judges are elected, many are appointed by the governors of their states. Bars (organizations of attorneys) sometimes recommend those members who would make good judges.

Attorneys for the losing side have a chance, before the end of the trial, to request that the trial be dismissed. They do this by asking the judge to set aside the verdict and to order a new trial. The request is called a **motion.** A reason must be given for each motion. The attorney may say that the judge applied the law in the wrong way, or that the jury made mistakes about the facts of the case, or that prejudicial statements have been made in the trial. It is up to the judge to grant or deny the motions made by the losing party's attorneys.

Rules of Evidence   The aim of the trial is to get at the truth by hearing and weighing the evidence that is presented about the case. The kind of evidence allowed in court and the way evidence is presented has been set down by **rules.** The rules have been made to see that both parties in a case are treated fairly. They also make sure that the jury will hear only evidence that is **relevant** to the case and that it is free from confusion and **fraud.**

Three rules of evidence used most often in trials are **competency of witnesses, privilege,** and **hearsay.** Competency of witnesses requires that witnesses be old enough or sane enough to be believable. A two-year-old baby and a seriously disturbed mental patient would not be competent witnesses. So, they would not be allowed to **testify** in a trial.

Privilege means that some parties may have such close relationships that one may not be required to testify about the other. These relationships include doctors and patients, lawyers and clients, husbands and

Relevant (REHL-uh-vunt) means related to, or connected with.

Fraud (FRAWD) is trickery which is used to injure another person in some way.

To **testify** (TESS-tuh-fie) means to state that something is true.

The confidential relationship between doctor and patient is recognized in a court of law. Therefore, a doctor is not required to give testimony about a patient.

wives. The rule of privilege may also be used to prevent information important to national security from being mentioned in court.

Hearsay is a statement said to have been made by someone who is not present at the trial. Such a statement cannot be used as evidence because the person cannot be cross-examined to see whether the statement was really made, or what was really meant by it. In special cases, the hearsay rule can be set aside. Such cases are mainly situations where the person who is said to have made a statement would be less likely to tell a lie—the last words of a dying person, for example.

Appeals   After the trial, the losing party has another chance to change the outcome. He or she may ask to make an **appeal** to a higher court. The reason for the appeal would be that the lower court made mistakes in applying the law to the case during the trial. The higher court may grant or deny the request for an appeal. It is not required to grant all such requests. However, when it denies the request it usually gives a reason.

The Appeals Court   An appeals court usually has three or more judges. The appeal is made in three stages. First, the judges consider the record of the trial in the lower court. Second, attorneys for both sides of the case present written statements called **briefs** to the court. Third, the attorneys argue their cases in person to the court. These arguments emphasize the points made in the briefs.

After considering the information presented to it, the appeals court may uphold (affirm) or reject (reverse) the lower court's verdict. Whatever the decision, it is based on majority rule. In case of a reversal, the appeals court may order a new trial in the lower court.

The Final Step   When the final appeals are over, the defendant will usually make the payment required by the court if he or she loses. If the party refuses to pay, his or her property may be sold to raise the money.

SECTION checkup

1. Is this statement true or false? One party to a civil suit is always a government.
2. What are the steps in a civil suit?
3. What are the steps in a civil trial?
4. List the three rules of evidence most often used. Give an example of each one.
5. What is an appeals court? What are the three stages of an appeal?

2. CONTRACTS

What Is a Contract? A contract is an agreement to do or not to do certain things. In a contract a person may agree to buy a car, sell a house, cut a lawn, or many other things. A person may also enter into a contract to stop doing something. For instance, someone may agree to stop selling goods in a community after the person has sold his or her business. A contract is also an agreement that can be **enforced in court.** This means that someone who has suffered from the breaking of a contract may sue the person who has broken the contract.

The Main Features of a Contract To be enforceable in court, a contract must have the following features:
1. Offer and acceptance
2. Genuine assent by the parties
3. Consideration
4. Legal in nature
5. Competent parties
6. In the form set down by law

The **offer** made in a contract must be definite. It must be meant to create a **binding** contract. Most advertisements are not offers because they are not meant to create binding agreements. They are invitations to make an agreement to buy the **goods** or **services** advertised. But, if you get an advertisement in the mail which asks you to subscribe to a magazine and you fill out the subscription coupon and send it back with your money, you are making a contract. The people who run the magazine must then send you the issues you have paid for. If they don't, they are breaking the contract.

Goods are things that are made for sale, such as cars, bicycles, radios. **Services** are actions done for money, such as mowing a lawn or delivering newspapers.

Both parties involved in a contract must agree on its terms. How is agreement expressed in this picture?

For most purposes, a minor is someone under the age of 18. With some exceptions, contracts with minors are not enforceable in court. The contracts are said to be **voidable.** This means that the minor may choose to perform his or her part of the agreement or not. If a minor chooses not to abide by the contract, he or she would have to give back any items obtained under the contract. Businesses usually will require parents to sign the contract of a minor. Thus the parents are responsible for upholding the terms of the contract if the minor does not.

Rules concerning contracts by minors vary from state to state. For instance, contracts by minors engaged in business are enforceable against minors in some states. Also, a minor may be required to repay the fair value of items such as food and clothing, even though the contract he or she made is not valid.

The **intent** (in-TENT) to have a binding agreement means the desire to have one.

The **acceptance** of an offer must be definite, too. And it must also be made with the **intent** to have a binding agreement. Furthermore, the acceptance must agree exactly with the offer. For example, if you offer to buy a high quality baseball for $4.50, a store cannot substitute a low quality ball for the same price. If it did this, it would be breaking a contract. Of course, if you decided to accept the low quality ball at the same price as the high quality ball, the contract would be real, or **valid.** An acceptance may be made in an informal way, by a nod of the head, or in a formal way, by a written paper.

Genuine (JEN-yew-in) means true or real. **Assent** (uh-SENT) means agreement.

Genuine assent depends on two things. First, the parties must actually want to enter into the contract. Second, they must freely come to an agreement. If one party tricks or threatens the other party, the contract is **void.**

Consideration is something of value that each party must agree to give as his or her part of the agreement. For instance, if you pay to see a movie, the movie theater must show it. As long as there is something of value given by each side, the court will not look at whether the things are equal in value unless fraud is committed by one of the parties. The main point is that each side must give something of value.

Void (VOYD) means empty. A void contract is one that has no legal value or power.

Contracts that are not legal in nature are those in which people make an agreement to harm another person, or to commit a crime. The courts will not enforce such contracts because they are against the public interest.

Competent (KOM-puh-tent) means able or capable.

To be valid, a contract must be made between **competent parties.** This means that people must be able to understand what they are doing and must be able to be held responsible for it legally. Because children and insane people are not able to fill either requirement, they cannot make binding contracts.

CASE STUDY

Contracts must also be prepared **in the form set down by law.** In most cases, an **oral agreement** is good and binding if the contract has all the other features needed to make it real and valid. However, there are certain types of contracts that must be in writing. For example, when a piece of land is given or sold by one person to another the agreement must be in writing.

Oral (ORE-ul) means spoken as opposed to written.

Breach of Contract   When one person does not do what he or she has agreed to do under the contract, **a breach of contract** occurs. If this happens, the injured party can enforce his or her rights in several ways. The injured party may sue for damages. That is, he or she may go to court to make the other party pay for failing to live up to the agreement. Another way is to cancel the contract and not perform any other acts under it. If the injured party does not want to cancel the contract or receive damages, he or she can sue in court to force the other party to abide by his or her part of the agreement. However, this can be done only when damages in the form of money are not enough to repay the injured party for losses.

CASE STUDY

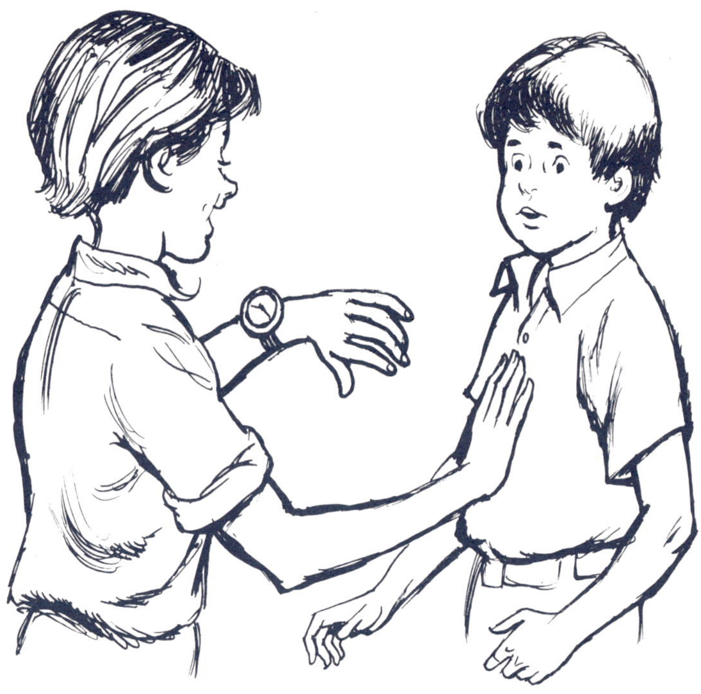

SECTION Checkup

1. What is a contract?
2. List the features that make a contract enforceable in court. Give an example of one feature.
3. What is **breach of contract**?
4. What can a person do to enforce his or her rights after a **breach of contract** has occurred?

3. TORTS

What Is a Tort?   A **tort** is a type of harm done by one person to another for which the harmed person may seek damages. But a tort is not a crime. This is because the injured party, not society as represented by the government, sues for the harm done. However, the same act may be both a tort and a crime. If this is so, the wrongdoer can be sued by the person hurt and also brought to trial and punished by the government. For example, if someone hit you with a club, you could sue that person and the government could **prosecute** the person.

Kinds of Torts　There are two kinds of torts: **intentional** and **unintentional,** or **negligent.** An intentional tort is an act that one intends to do which may forseeably cause an injury. Suppose you are the star player of your tennis team. Your team is about to play Team X for the local championship. If a member of Team X knocks you down with a bike so that you won't be able to play in the championship match, that person would be committing an **intentional tort.** Of course, before you could collect damages, you would have to prove in court that he or she really meant to hurt you.

An unintentional or negligent tort is a harmful act done without being careful of the rights of others. Unlike an intentional tort, the person doing the harm may not mean to do it. It may be done accidentally, or it may be the result of carelessness. Under the law, a person has a duty

Would purse-snatching be considered an assault or a battery? Why?

to use care with the person and property of others. If carelessness results in harm to another person, the other person may be able to sue. An example of an unintentional tort often seen today is an automobile accident in which one party has been driving carelessly and harms another.

Paralegals

Paralegals (lawyer's assistants) help attorneys in a variety of ways. Their duties vary from office to office. These assistants may help investigate cases, interview witnesses, manage the office, complete forms, and do legal research.

Paralegals gain the training or experience needed for the position in a variety of ways. Some take college or business school courses and some enroll in special paralegal schools. Others gain experience performing certain tasks in other jobs. For example, while working as a police officer a paralegal could have learned how to investigate a case.

Kinds of Intentional Torts   Assault, battery, and defamation are the three kinds of intentional torts. An **assault** occurs when someone is made to fear that he or she is in immediate danger of being harmed by someone else. Thrusting a stick in the direction of another person would be an assault if the person could show in court that he or she was in fear of being harmed right away. He or she would also have to show, however, that the person holding the stick had the ability to injure. If a three-year-old child thrust a stick at a husky teenager, the child's parents could not be sued. Even though the teenager might have felt in danger of being hurt, the parents could show that the child did not have the ability to hurt.

When someone pokes or jabs another with a stick, a **battery** has been committed because the stick touched the person's body. But the person touched must show that there was intent to harm and that there was no reason for touching. If you jab someone with a stick to defend yourself from a similar or greater harm, you probably can't be sued, because you had a good reason for touching.

Defamation means making statements that are meant to harm someone by ruining their reputation. Defamation may be false oral statements—**slander**—or written false statements—**libel.**

In order to recover damages for defamation, the injured party must prove certain things. First, he or she must show that a false statement really was made and spread about. Second, the injured party must prove that the statement caused harm to his or her reputation. Third, he or she must show that damages resulted from the statement.

Unintentional Torts   A court may decide that someone should pay damages for hurting another, even though no harm was intended. When this happens, the person who did the harm is said to have committed an **unintentional tort** by acting **negligently.** For negligence to be proved, the injured person must prove four things. First, he or she must prove that the wrongdoer had a duty to be careful, and second, that the wrongdoer was not careful. Third, the injured party must show that lack of care directly caused harm to him or her. Fourth, it must be proven that a certain amount of damage resulted from the harm.

To act **negligently** (NEG-luh-gent-lee) is to act carelessly in a way that causes harm.

CASE STUDY

Trudy Careful was driving her car down Main Street, with Harry Hurry driving very closely behind. A cat ran out in front of Trudy's car. When Trudy braked, Harry ran into the back of her car. The court decided in Trudy's favor. It ruled that Harry was negligent in following too closely. He could forsee that Trudy might have to stop suddenly, so he should have remained a safe distance behind her.

To decide how much care one person owes to another, the court uses a simple measuring tool. It determines how much care an average individual would use in the same situation. During the trial, the jury must decide this. Or, if the parties have agreed not to have a trial, the judge will make a decision.

Defenses   The wrongdoer may avoid paying the injured person if he or she can show a defense. A defense can be shown in several ways. The wrongdoer may show that the injured person was not reasonably careful and so was partly responsible for the injury. For instance the wrongdoer might be able to show that someone injured in an automobile accident was driving too fast on a wet road and, so, helped cause the accident.

Another defense is to show that the injured person **assumed the risk.** A risk is assumed when someone enters into a dangerous situation knowing that harm might result. An example of this would be accepting a ride in a car with someone who is drunk.

Usually, minors are responsible for their torts. However, in unintentional torts, courts usually consider the age and experience of the minor.

Parents are usually not responsible for the torts of their minor children. But they might be responsible in cases where they have told children to do something wrong, or have approved a child's wrongful act. If parents have given a child a dangerous instrument such as a rifle, and have not shown him or her how to use it safely, they might be responsible for damage done with it.

A **statute** (STA-chewt) is a law passed by the legislature.

The Statute of Limitations   State laws require that people sue for injuries from torts within a certain period of time. This type of law is known as a **statute of limitations.** It may limit the time for beginning a suit to within one year from the date the harm was done.

To **compensate** (KOM-pen-sayt) means to pay someone for something.

Damages   If the court decides that someone is the victim of a tort, damages may be awarded to the injured party. These damages can cover expenses caused by the injury, such as hospital bills, and the physical injury itself, such as the loss of an eye. Damages may also be awarded for pain suffered and for losses the victim may suffer in the future as a result of the injury. For instance, if an injury meant that someone would be unable to work for a living, he or she would receive damages for this harm. These damages are said to **compensate** the victim. In addition, the court may award an additional amount of money to the victim. These damages are meant to punish the wrongdoer who has acted **maliciously** in causing the harm.

To act **maliciously** (muh-LISH-us-lee) is to act wickedly or with an evil purpose.

SECTION CHECKUP

1. What is a tort?
2. Give three examples of intentional torts.
3. What must someone do to recover damages for defamation?
4. What must be proved to show that a person acted negligently?
5. What two defenses may a wrongdoer use to avoid paying the injured person?
6. What is meant by a **statute of limitations?**

4. PROTECTING THE CONSUMER AND THE ENVIRONMENT

In the last twenty years or so, a new branch of the law has developed. It is known as **consumer law.** The idea of protecting consumers has roots deep in our past. People have always believed that sellers should not cheat their customers. At the beginning of this century people started and joined movements to protect consumers from such wrongdoing. Nevertheless, it was only recently that enough statutes were passed to make consumer law a separate branch of civil law.

Who Is a Consumer?   Everyone is a consumer, because all of us have many needs and wants and we buy goods and services to satisfy them. We consume goods such as food and clothes, and services such as mail delivery and entertainment. We depend on those who provide goods and services to give us things in good condition and in the form paid for.

Consumers buy goods and services to satisfy needs or desires. What needs or desires are these consumers satisfying?

What Rights Do Consumers Have?   When we are disappointed in the goods and services we receive, we have a right to do several things. We can make a complaint in court, or in an office set up to receive consumers' complaints. We can refuse damaged goods or refuse to pay for poor services. Of course, sellers of the goods and services also have the right to defend themselves against these actions.

Consumers and Contracts   Do you remember the features of a legal contract? Much of the protection that the law gives to consumers comes from these requirements. A contract between a consumer and a seller must meet the requirements of offer and acceptance. Consumers are also protected by laws against **breach of contract.** Laws relating to torts offer protection, too. If someone is negligent in performing services, the consumer can make a complaint.

Consumers are also protected by something called the Uniform Commercial Code. It is a set of laws that has been passed, in some form, by the governments of nearly all states. The Uniform Commercial Code includes safety measures for consumers called **sales contracts.** These contracts state clearly who—buyer or seller—takes the risk when goods are damaged after the time of the sale. They also state exactly when consumers become the legal owner of goods or services they have bought.

Warranties also Protect Consumers   A warranty is a guarantee for goods sold. Warranties say, for example, that if a consumer buys

something that turns out to be damaged, he or she can return it to the seller or maker. They might also say that the maker will repair something that breaks down within so many days after it has been bought.

Warranties may be **express** or **implied.** An express warranty is a statement made by the seller about some feature of the goods. For example, an express warranty can state that a light bulb is guaranteed to burn for 200 hours. Often, express warranties are in writing. An implied warranty is one that is not stated in so many words by the seller, but it applies to the sale by law. For instance, all sellers are supposed to give buyers complete ownership of the goods sold. If a seller fails to meet these warranties, he or she can be sued in court.

Warranties cover many other things, too. They guarantee that something is suited to the purpose for which it is sold; that a stereo will play records, or that foods are fit to be eaten by humans.

"Let the Buyer Beware."   An old rule of law that applies to consumers is **caveat emptor.** These are Latin words that mean "let the buyer beware." The rule applies in cases when the buyer has had enough time to inspect the goods and the seller does not use fraud in the sale. Under the rule of **caveat emptor,** the buyer can risk loss. This is why new laws, like the Uniform Commercial Code, were made to give consumers more protection.

How Consumers are Protected   The law has several ways of protecting consumers who have been harmed by faulty goods or services. Tort law allows consumers to recover damages for the negligence of the maker or the seller. Contract law permits consumers to sue if a maker or seller has broken warranties which are implied by the law.

The citizen as consumer is protected in other ways. Under the Food, Drug, and Cosmetics Act of the federal government, certain **additives** to foods, drugs, and cosmetics are forbidden. They are believed to threaten people with possible harm. Other federal laws protect children from unsafe toys. Makers of goods must not mislabel food, drugs, and other items used in the home, and people who lend money must state in writing how much **interest** the borrower has to pay.

State legislatures have also passed laws to protect consumers. They have given various state officers the task of looking after the interests of consumers. Many of these laws require that a state official represent the people at hearings where **public utilities** ask for price increases.

Many communities have taken action to protect consumers, too. They have offices where consumers can complain about receiving poor goods or services. The Better Business Bureau, for example, is a private organization set up to handle complaints of consumers. It has offices in most communities.

Consumers, however, are supposed to act responsibly in making purchases. They should inspect goods, question the seller, and shop around to find the best item. They should be careful when making a

Additives (ADD-uh-tives) are chemicals mixed with foods, drugs, or cosmetics to preserve them, make them look better, or taste a certain way.

Interest (IN-trust) is the amount people pay to a bank or a person for borrowing money.

Public utilities (yew-TILL-uh-tees) are companies that provide electricity, gas, water, and other such services to the people of an area.

purchase for another reason. While the law protects them, it often takes a lot of time and money to go to court when you have been harmed by poor goods or services.

SECTION checkup

1. What do these terms mean: warranty, **caveat emptor.**
2. How does the Uniform Commercial Code protect consumers?
3. How are consumers protected by **tort law** and **contract law?**

5. PROTECTING THE ENVIRONMENT

Environmental law is another new branch of civil law. Like consumer law, it has grown during the past twenty years. Our environment is our surroundings—the air, land, and water around us. In a very simple society with few people, the environment is harmed mostly by natural forces such as lightning, fires, floods, winds, or lack of water. In our complex society, with many people, it is harmed mostly by human actions. We dirty our air and water. We use land in ways that result in overcrowding, littering, or poisoning of the soil. We cause harm by making too much noise. There are so many more of us every day that we risk using up the space there is to live in and the things we need to live on.

The Government Takes Action For years, Americans have fought to protect our **natural resources** and to preserve open land, clean air, and clean water. But, in the 1960s and 1970s, the federal government and state governments passed many new laws about the environment.

Some of the most important laws passed by the federal government are the three that follow.

1. **The National Environmental Policy Act of 1969.** With this act, the federal government, state and local governments, and private groups declared that they would protect the environment. Part of this act says that government must describe how actions it is going to take will affect the environment. By this act, Congress also set up the Council on Environmental Quality. Its job is to advise the President on environmental matters. The act also established the Environmental Protection Agency. The **agency** has the power to protect air and water and to deal with such serious problems as getting rid of solid waste.

2. **The Clean Air Amendments.** With this law, the Environmental Protection Agency established standards for the quality of our air.

An **agency** (AY-jun-see) is a group, or office, with the power to take action on something.

Factories are often responsible for destroying the quality of air.

The states are supposed to see to it that the air is the quality it should be. For example, states are required to have laws that control exhaust fumes from automobiles.

    3. **The Federal Water Pollution Control Act.** The Environmental Protection Agency also declared that our water should be of good quality. Here, too, the states have been given the responsibility for cleaning up the environment. Under this act, they are supposed to see that pollution of **navigable** waters is stopped by 1985. This act also allows the federal government to give money to communities to build plants for getting rid of **solid waste.**

    Look over these three laws again. What things do they have in common? First of all, the laws require the federal and state governments, along with local communities, to unite in fighting pollution. Second, the federal government offers communities money to improve the environment.

Navigable (NAV-uh-guh-bl) waters are those that can be crossed by ships or other sailing vessels.

Solid waste is waste that flows into the sewer system.

To **lobby** (LAHB-ee) means to try to influence members of government to vote for something by writing letters or talking with them personally.

Citizens Take Action   Over the years, many individual citizens and groups of citizens have taken action to protect the environment. The methods they have used to do this are varied. In the early 1970s, people took unusual actions to call attention to problems. They held large demonstrations and rallies. Sometimes they even did things that were illegal and were arrested and jailed for them.

Recently, people have acted less dramatically. But their actions have had results, too. With the help of lawyers who specialize in environmental law, they have brought lawsuits against polluters. They have **lobbied** in Congress and in state governments and have started campaigns to tell the public about environmental problems.

For some time, environmentalists have known that group action gets the best results. Today, there are about three thousand groups devoted to protecting the environment. Most of them work on the local level. Three groups that are active across the nation are the Sierra Club, the Environmental Defense Fund, and the Isaak Walton League. The Sierra Club works mostly to save wilderness areas. The Environmental Defense Fund provides money for lawsuits to protect the environment. And the Isaak Walton League tries to protect both wilderness areas and public lands.

A Many-sided Question   Many groups and individuals are committed to protecting the environment. But it is not a simple problem with simple solutions. Many of the ways in which we use—and harm—our environment are necessary to our way of life. For instance, people demand goods and services which can be made or delivered only in ways that do some environmental damage. Automobiles and buses cause serious air pollution, but no one would think of doing without them. The mining and burning of coal also threaten the environment, but coal must be used for energy, because other forms of energy are becoming scarce. Also, when factories or mines are shut down to improve air quality, many people lose their jobs.

Providing goods and services in ways that protect the environment often cost more to the consumer. For example, bottling soft drinks in returnable containers can raise the price of the soft drinks, and adding pollution controls to cars makes cars more expensive.

People also object to laws that say how land can be used or how much noise you can make. They feel that their land is theirs to use as they wish and that noise pollution laws limit their freedom of speech.

As you can see, protecting the environment is not an easy matter. It is very difficult and very complex. For this reason, both sides—environmentalists and producers of goods and services—need the help of specialists. They must turn constantly to people who are experts in the field of environmental law.

SECTION Checkup

1. List the names of three important laws passed by the federal government to protect the environment.
2. Describe one of these laws.
3. What two things do these laws have in common?
4. Describe some problems involved in protecting the environment.

How is this young man fighting against pollution?

CHAPTER REVIEW

Our courts and legal system have many tasks to perform. One of these tasks is to resolve conflicts among individuals and groups. In order to settle disputes the courts have developed special ways of trying cases. These are used each time a suit is brought. They are designed to protect the rights of all the parties involved in the suit.

Most disputes arise from **breach of contract** or from some form of **tort.** To be valid, contracts must contain various elements such as **offer and acceptance.** Torts must have certain features, too. These include either **intentional harm** or **negligence.**

Two branches of the law that have developed in recent years are **consumer law** and **environmental law.** Consumer law is meant to protect people who purchase goods and services. Environmental law is designed to protect air, water, and land. However, it is a difficult and complicated branch of the law. This is because the need to protect the environment often conflicts with the citizen's need to produce and consume goods and services.

We live in a complex society where various types of individuals and groups have different wants and desires. It is the task of the civil side of the law to settle disputes among these individuals and groups so that we may live as harmoniously as possible.

QUESTIONS FOR REVIEW

1. What legal steps take place after an injury occurs and before the actual trial begins?
2. What education must someone have to be a judge? a lawyer? What other requirements must they fulfill?
3. What does a paralegal do?
4. What is a privileged relationship?
5. Must all contracts be in writing?
6. What are **unintentional** or **negligent** torts?
7. What tactics have citizens used over the years to try to protect the environment?

1. Draft a Simple Contract. With your classmates, divide into groups of three. Half of the groups are to write simple contracts which include all of the required features. Your contract may be about providing goods—cakes, fish, vegetables, toys; or about providing services—shoveling snow, sweeping sidewalks, washing windows. Or, you may write a contract about not doing something, for example, agreeing not to mow lawns in a certain neighborhood. The other groups are to be three-judge courts. They will review the contracts and decide whether they meet the requirements necessary for a contract to be enforceable in court.

2. Torts-in-Class. Members of your class will be asked to show how various torts occur. Each class member is responsible for seeing that no student is harmed. You can make up your own torts, or you can use these: (a) When someone accidentally bumps into you, yell loudly at that person and move toward him or her with fists raised (**assault**). (b) Hit a classmate lightly on the upper arm (**battery**). (c) Tell one classmate that another still sleeps with a teddy bear (**slander**). (d) Accidentally step on the foot of a classmate (**unintentional tort**). (e) Borrow a piece of chalk from a classmate, then drop it and break it (**negligence**). Discuss each action to see why it is a tort.

your law library

Fisk, McKee, and Norbert J. Mietus, *Applied Business Law, Eleventh Edition.* Cincinnati: South-Western Publishing Company, 1977.

Loeb, Robert H., Jr., *Your Legal Rights as a Minor.* New York: Franklin Watts, Inc., 1974.

Murphy, Earl F., *Man and His Environment: Law.* New York: Harper and Row, 1971.

Norwick, Kenneth P., ed., *Your Legal Rights: Making the Law Work for You.* New York: The John Day Company, 1973.

THE BILL OF RIGHTS

amendment (uh-
MEND-ment) an
amendment is a
change in a
document.

Not all of the founders of our government felt that the Constitution in its original form guaranteed the people the rights for which they had fought the British. Therefore, they demanded that a list of these rights be added to the Constitution. The list is called the Bill of Rights. It is made up of the first ten **amendments** to the Constitution.

Several rights are listed in the first ten amendments including freedom of religion, speech, assembly, the right to a fair trial, and to life, liberty, and property. Among the most important is the right to freedom of speech, which is guaranteed by the First Amendment. Our ability to live peacefully together and to reach important decisions depends on the existence of this freedom. There are limits on freedom of speech in order to prevent violations of the rights of individuals and damage to the general welfare.

Since the founding of the country, other amendments have been added. In a democracy such as the United States, the government is ruled by the will of the majority. However, there are cases when this places a hardship on the minority. As additions were made to the Constitution through the Amendments, protection was given to the minority. They were guaranteed equal grievances. Minorities have not always enjoyed equal protection. The most prominent of these groups has been Black Americans. They were guaranteed citizenship after the Civil War, but only in recent years have they begun to gain the full protection the Constitution promises to all citizens.

Discrimination in public places has been declared unconstitutional. The Supreme Court and Congress have attempted to end discrimination in the sale or rental of housing.

The government has still tried to keep church and state separate by prohibiting acts such as prayer in public schools. The government allows people to practice the religion of their choice as long as others are not harmed by it.

To know the meaning of the Bill of Rights and to be able to describe some of the rights it guarantees.

To describe the role of freedom of speech in a democratic society and to be able to explain some of the limitations on this right and the reasons for them.

To describe the relationship between the majority and the minority in a democratic society.

To know some of the ways in which a minority can gain and protect its rights in a democratic society.

To know the meaning of equal protection in a democratic society.

To be able to describe some of the ways in which minorities in the United States have gained equal protection of their rights under the law.

CHAPTER PREVIEW

1. FUNDAMENTAL FREEDOMS
2. FREEDOM OF SPEECH
3. MAJORITY RULE AND MINORITY RIGHTS
4. EQUAL PROTECTION

---

1. FUNDAMENTAL FREEDOMS

After the Constitution of the United States was ratified in 1789, the country's leaders still did not feel that the fundamental freedoms they wanted were specifically guaranteed. Therefore, these freedoms were identified and expressed in the first ten amendments to the Constitution. These amendments became known as the Bill of Rights. In later years, other amendments have been passed to guarantee both additional freedoms and the equality of citizens within this nation.

The First Amendment The First Amendment begins with the phrase, "Congress shall make no law respecting an establishment of religion, or prohibiting the free exercise thereof." This statement was meant to make sure that there would not be one state religion in this country, as was the case in most European countries. Many colonists had come to this country so that they could practice the religion of their choice. They did not want their new government to have the power to take away their freedom of worship.

The First Amendment and Religion   Most of the concern today about the possible establishment of a state religion has involved the public schools. All Americans must attend school for a certain number of years. The United States Supreme Court has taken action several times to prevent public schools from teaching any specific religion in the classroom.

As a result of the decisions made by the Supreme Court, a public school cannot have a reading of the Bible or a recitation of the Lord's Prayer. A school may not permit people to use public buildings during the school day to provide religious instruction, even if it is done on a voluntary basis. It is legal, however, to allow students to leave school and go to another site for religious instruction. A state may not stop the teaching of Darwin's theory of evolution just because it seems to conflict with the account of the creation in the Bible. These are but a few of the many important issues that have been decided by the Court in an effort to keep the separation of church and state.

Pictured are Clarence Darrow (left) and William Jennings Bryan (right). In 1925 Darrow defended John Scopes, who was teaching evolution to his students. Bryan was against these teachings.

ONE STEP BEYOND—
OLD ORDER AMISH MENNONITE CHURCH

The Amish are made up of the followers of Jakob Amman, a Swiss Mennonite bishop who withdrew from the Mennonite Church in 1693. The Amish live in several places in the United States, including Lancaster County, Pennsylvania; Holmes County, Ohio; and Elkhart, Indiana. All Amish wear plain clothes. The men have beards and the women wear bonnets and shawls. The children dress in clothes similar to those of their parents. The Amish still travel by horse and buggy. Their religious services are held in private homes. They speak a form of German commonly known as Pennsylvania Dutch. The Amish raise their children in a very strict environment in an effort to keep the values and morals set by their religion. They have always been fearful of relationships between their children and non-Amish neighbors. It is believed that these relationships lead to the lowering of religious standards. They feel that their children require only a basic education with little need for secondary school training. They also believe that too much schooling will lead to exposure of their children to worldly activities that could harm their Christian values. The issue of whether Amish children had to attend high school was decided by the Supreme Court in 1972 in the case of <u>Wisconsin</u> v. <u>Yoder</u>. The court ruled that the state of Wisconsin could not make the Amish send their children to school beyond the eighth grade.

The Amish believe in a simple life and wear very plain clothes even today.

The freedom of speech clause of the First Amendment is concerned with preventing a state religion. It is also concerned with preventing the government from interfering with the freedom to worship or not to worship as one pleases. The Supreme Court has agreed that a citizen has the absolute right to any or no religious belief. However, the right to practice a religious belief has given rise to many controversial questions. The Court has generally ruled that the practice of religious beliefs must not go against the public peace, health, safety, and morals. For example, the Court ruled that Mormons must stop their traditional practice of having more than one wife. The Court also ruled that all children, including those of Christian Scientists, must obey laws that require vaccination before entering school. On the other hand, the Court has supported many religious groups. For example, it has upheld the right of Jehovah's Witnesses and others to refuse to participate in the Pledge of Allegiance. It has also protected the right of parents to send their children to religious schools.

The First Amendment and the Press   Another important guarantee in the First Amendment is freedom of the press. This freedom has been broadened to include not only newspapers but also television, radio, movies, and other communications media. The guarantee has caused problems, however. The press has been criticized for being free to say whatever it chooses about important issues and candidates. An especially touchy problem has arisen when a newspaper attacks a person and then refuses to allow that person to respond to the charges. To deal with this problem, the state of Florida passed a law which required newspapers to provide free space for replies by candidates for public office who had been criticized by the newspaper. However, this law was declared unconstitutional by the Supreme Court. In fact, the general attitude of the Court toward the press has been one of almost total support of editorial policy.

The press must make every effort to insure that what it writes is not based on a falsehood which will injure a person's reputation. If the press prints or broadcasts something harmful to a person's reputation, that person can sue for libel.

Before statements made about public officials can be considered libelous, it must be proven that the statements were made with a knowledge of their falsity or with reckless disregard for whether they were true or false. In cases dealing with private citizens the court has ruled that states can allow damage awards for libelous falsehoods if there is evidence of negligence or fault. However, these damages must be limited to compensation for actual injury to the person or to the person's reputation.

The press and other news media have the responsibility to keep people informed. In recent years, they have informed the American public about important issues such as the civil rights movement, space exploration, and Watergate.

Freedom of Assembly and Petition   The First Amendment also gives citizens of this nation the right to peaceful assembly and **petition.** They can meet in groups to discuss issues of their choice as long as the assembly is peaceful. Meetings can be held in private homes, meeting halls, public streets and parks. However, people cannot do anything they wish under the pretense of using freedom of peaceful assembly and petition. They are not free to incite riots, block traffic, take over schools, seize and hold the office of a mayor or a university chancellor, or make speeches in public streets during rush hours. The Supreme Court has ruled that the government may make reasonable regulations about time, place, and manner of assemblies and petitions in order to preserve order.

On the other hand, the Court has not given the government a free hand to maintain order in public meetings. The government must do this by following laws that are fairly drawn, evenly administered, and that take into account differing points of view. In cases where local

Citizens of the United States have the right to assemble peacefully. They are not free to riot. Martin Luther King, Jr., was known for his peaceful gatherings.

governments have made rules about public meetings or do not follow lawful existing rules, the Court has ruled in favor of the demonstrators.

Public facilities such as libraries, courthouses, schools, and parks can be used for peaceful assemblies. However, if the assembly turns into a situation that interferes with regular programs in the facilities, a state has the constitutional authority to punish wrongdoers.

The Court has also made it quite clear that the right to assemble and petition does not include the right to trespass on privately-owned property. In this situation, the state may act to protect the rights of the owners of the property. Therefore, the Court has carefully examined cases of confrontations by the police and demonstrators. In this manner it tries to make sure that the purpose of the right to assemble and petition as stated in the First Amendment is carried out.

The Second Amendment Another freedom that has been kept by the people is the right to keep and bear arms. It is guaranteed by the Second Amendment. At the period of history when the Bill of Rights was ratified, the people had just gained their independence from what they considered to be a tyrannical government. They wanted to be able to keep and bear arms in order to insure that this would never happen again. They also needed guns for protection and hunting for food.

Problems with the Second Amendment   In recent years, the right to keep and bear arms has been the object of a great deal of concern. The assassinations of John F. Kennedy, Martin Luther King, and Robert Kennedy showed how easy it was to get a weapon. They also showed the harmful ways in which these weapons could be used. As a result, there has been a strong movement toward gun control; there has been an equally strong movement against it.

At this point, little has been done to affect the intent of this amendment. The only legislation has been the Gun Control Act of 1968. This act states that interstate mail order sales of all firearms and ammunition are prohibited. Unsuccessful attempts have been made to require all persons owning guns to register them.

The Ninth Amendment   The Ninth Amendment was intended to make sure that the people would always be able to designate needed rights. Therefore, it was declared that the fact that a certain right is not mentioned in the Constitution does not mean that the right does not exist.

Robert F. Kennedy was assassinated in 1968 during his campaign for President.

The authors of the Bill of Rights tried to take the future into account in creating this amendment. They realized that it was not possible for them to identify all the rights citizens might feel were necessary at a later date. This amendment has been used to justify the passage of additional amendments guaranteeing specific freedoms not specified in the first ten amendments.

SECTION Checkup

1. Why did the founders of our government insist on an amendment to the Constitution that guaranteed freedom of religion?
2. Under what circumstances may the press be sued for libel?
3. To what extent can persons use public streets and parks for meetings?
4. What do you think is the effect of the Gun Control Act of 1968?

2. FREEDOM OF SPEECH

Democracy and Freedom of Speech   If a government is to be a true democracy it must act to protect the expression of all types of opinions. It must even act to insure that unhappy citizens are able to express their criticisms of the government without fear of arrest. To do otherwise would mean abandoning democracy in favor of **authoritarian** rule. The First Amendment to the Constitution says, among other things, "Congress shall make no law...abridging the freedom of speech..." What exactly does this mean? Are there to be any allowable restrictions on freedom of speech? Why is freedom of speech so important?

The Free Market of Ideas   How is any person to know what is true about worldwide political matters? In authoritarian countries the citizens must follow political leaders without question. In a democracy, citizens have the right to form their own opinions about political matters. This right is made a reality by the existence of freedom of speech. Anyone with a new political idea has the right to be heard. If the new idea is powerful, others might adopt it as their opinion. The new idea might then be used to solve problems in the political marketplace. If the idea is weak or not needed, the idea will probably die a natural death.

authoritarian (aw-thor-i-TARE-ee-un) authoritarian rule is one which stresses unquestioning obedience to a ruler or government rather than individual liberty and democratic participation in government.

Constitutional Amendments and Free Speech Every modern amendment to the Constitution of the United States has won acceptance in an open marketplace of political ideas. However, many proposed amendments have failed to win acceptance. One amendment was declared unconstitutional after it had been in effect for nearly 14 years. This amendment, the Eighteenth, made it against the law to produce, sell, or transport alcoholic beverages in the United States. It was ratified in 1919 and remained in force until 1933 when the Twenty-first Amendment repealed it.

During this span of time, what appeared to be a good political idea was adopted, tried out, found to be unworkable, and was ultimately rejected. These changes were made without violence or bloodshed. Freedom of speech in the form of debates made the peaceful change possible.

The latest amendment to be discussed is the Equal Rights Amendment (ERA). It proposes to establish a legal guarantee that women will have and be able to exercise the same political and economic rights as men. Supporters argue that the amendment is needed to help abolish

This federal agent destroys smuggled liquor during the Prohibition era.

discrimination against women. Opponents argue that the amendment is not needed since discrimination is already illegal. They contend that the ERA would make laws giving special benefits to women impossible. This means that the ERA would remove protections that women now have. An example of this is that women and men might use the same public restrooms. Many citizens feel that total equality of the sexes would be an ideal condition. Others feel that basic differences between women and men exist and must be recognized when laws are passed. Freedom of speech allows a "great debate" about ERA to continue. Eventually, ERA will win acceptance or be rejected. Everyone who wishes to express ideas on the subject will have been heard. As a result, the decision for or against ERA will probably be accepted by most of the general public.

The Supreme Court and Free Speech   Freedom of speech applies not only to great political debates such as the ones concerning prohibition or ERA, but also to many matters which are part of the everyday life of all citizens. All citizens have a set of beliefs. Some of these beliefs are expressed by speaking; others are expressed by acting. Since it first began to rule on cases involving the First Amendment, the Supreme Court has allowed the government to regulate some of these freedoms, such as freedom of speech. To guide this regulation the Court must distinguish between constitutional and unconstitutional **restraints** on a citizen's right to exercise freedom of speech and other First Amendment freedoms. In deciding what is and what is not unconstitutional restraint upon any of the First Amendment freedoms, the Court follows the general policy of distinguishing between beliefs and actions. Any citizen may believe anything, but the court has restrained actions which would be harmful to other individuals or to the general welfare of all citizens.

In ruling on cases involving freedom of speech, the Court has usually treated speaking as being halfway between believing and acting. Thus, freedom of expression has never been treated as an **absolute** right. Usually the Court has felt that it is more difficult for a citizen to violate another citizen's rights or harm the general welfare by speaking. Only that type of freedom of expression that does not **infringe** on the rights of individuals, minorities, or the general welfare is protected by the First Amendment. Those types of freedom of expression that infringe on the rights of others are not protected and can be prohibited by law. It is usually these laws that constitutionally restrain certain types of speech that touch the daily lives of all of us.

Restraints on Free Speech   The Supreme Court found in the case of *Schenck* vs. *United States* in 1919 that Congress and other legislative bodies have the right to make laws that restrain types of speech that create a "clear and present danger." Suppose you were sitting in a crowded theater and decided to exercise your right to freedom of speech by yelling, "Fire! Fire! Fire!," when no fire existed. Laws prohibiting such actions are constitutional because the cry of "Fire!" causes a clear and present danger of injury to panic-stricken people rushing to get away from a fire that does not exist. In an open field where people could look around to see if a fire really existed, such a speech might be regarded as a harmless prank rather than a violation of law.

To prove the constitutionality of a law restraining speech, the government must prove that whatever speech is prohibited would be unpopular or even dangerous. They would also have to prove that the speech actually creates a dangerous condition which the government has the duty to prevent. This dangerous condition is usually personal injury to the speaker or to those hearing the speaker. Laws making "inciting a riot" illegal are constitutional, but a citizen does not violate them simply by making unpopular statements in public. A real danger of injury must be present before speech can be legally stopped by the police.

Expressing Unpopular Political Ideas   The expression of unpopular political opinions has always posed a problem for government officials in the United States. Suppose a few people in a city where there is a state-supported university want to invite a known racist to make a public speech in an on-campus auditorium. This auditorium belongs to the people of the state. A majority of these people may not approve of such a speaker or the content of his or her speech. Suppose

Many people were against the Vietnam War. However, they did have the right to express their opinions.

the legislature of the state makes a law denying use of the auditorium to speakers who are members of unpopular groups. Would such a law be constitutional?

The Supreme Court has never looked with favor upon laws establishing "prior restraint" upon freedom of speech. This means that the Court has seldom allowed a local, state, or even the federal government to rule in advance that persons or groups may not express their views. Neither may particular views, even views critical of the government, be stopped. Only in clear cases of national security interests may laws restrain the expression of information in advance. For example, regulations requiring a review of the content of a speech before its delivery in public are not constitutional. This is true even in the case of school regulations giving administrators or teachers authority to review in advance student speeches made during assemblies or graduations.

Two rights are protected by the Supreme Court's refusal to allow "prior restraint." First, those persons wishing to express unpopular opinions may do so. Second, members of the public, even though they may be in a minority, are able to exercise the right to hear the expression of all types of opinions. Therefore all types of these opinions can be evaluated as to their political or social value.

Slander   Other examples of how a legal restraint of speech touches our everyday lives are the laws against slander. No individual may damage or destroy the reputation of another person by making untrue public statements about that person intentionally. This law protects professional people in law, medicine, teaching, and other fields from untrue charges of incompetence made orally by their dissatisfied clients. It protects all citizens from untrue charges of a personal nature that might be made orally by neighbors or people that they know.

CASE STUDY

Suppose the Jones family keeps their show dog at a kennel. If the kennel owner and the Joneses disagree about the price being charged, the Joneses may be angry with the owner. If the Joneses then try to destroy the owner's reputation as a good kennel operator by saying falsely to his customers that he cursed in front of their children or that he was cruel to their dog, they may be guilty of slander. Their right to freedom of speech does not extend so far as to make it legal for them to harm another person's reputation or business by telling falsehoods about that person intentionally.

Conclusion   In its long history the Supreme Court has developed guidelines for deciding cases involving freedom of speech. Saying words that actually cause harm to others or that violate the rights of individuals can be restrained by law. Criticizing the government or saying words that are unpopular or cause hurt feelings cannot be legally restrained. Prior restraint of expression is hardly ever legal. In deciding individual cases the judges make unique decisions, basing their opinions on such facts as: What was said? Where was it said? What intent did the speaker have? What circumstances surround the speech? What type of government—local, state, or federal—attempted to restrain the speech? Was the restraint prior to the speech? What reasons for restraining the speech existed? Only when the answers to such questions show that a speaker's words have caused actions that result in real harm to others may freedom of speech be restrained.

SECTION Checkup

1. How does the phrase "clear and present danger" relate to a person's right to exercise freedom of speech?
2. Why can't the government exercise "prior restraint" in its regulation of freedom of speech?
3. Why is the "free market of ideas" important to the existence of democracy?
4. What is the purpose of the Ninth Amendment?
5. What other First Amendment freedom is closely related to freedom of speech?
6. How are freedom of speech and the adoption or rejection of a Constitutional amendment related?

---

3. MAJORITY RULE AND MINORITY RIGHTS

What is a democracy? One simple answer is an association of people who rule themselves by group decisions arrived at by voting. Suppose you are a member of a small group of 200 people who set out to rule themselves. Would you agree to obey whatever laws this group made? You might agree, provided you knew your vote would count the same as everyone else's. You might agree, provided that the democratic principle of majority rule was to be used when the voting took place.

Majority Rule Majority rule means that when a vote is taken on a proposed law, the proposed law will be adopted only if "half plus one" of those participating vote for the law. If your group of 200 votes on a proposed law, it will pass if at least 101 votes are cast in favor of it. The United States is an association of over 200 million people who have agreed to rule themselves by voting on important group decisions. We call ourselves a democracy because, when the voting takes place, everyone's vote counts the same and the outcome of any vote is determined by the principle of majority rule.

The Plight of a Minority Suppose you were one of only 20 redheaded people in a self-governing group of 200 people who have agreed to abide by the principles of one person, one vote, and majority rule. One day the group meets and discusses what to do about a shortage of food. A non-redheaded person proposes a law saying that red-

A show of raised hands is a very common way of taking a vote.

headed persons should be allowed to eat only two meals a day instead of three. How would you feel? How would you vote? What if many of the non-redheaded persons in the group of 200 felt that the proposal to limit redheads to two meals a day was a good one? It would save just enough food to take care of the shortage. A vote was taken, and the proposal passed by a majority of 180 to 20. It became a law. The food-store manager had to comply with the law by selling only enough food for two meals a day to redheaded people.

After a few months, the food shortage disappeared. In a group meeting, you propose a vote to do away with the law limiting redheads to two meals a day. A non-redhead proposed to keep the law and add a provision to sell the extra food to anyone who was not a redhead and who could afford to pay for it. Your proposal to abolish the new law lost on a vote of 150 to 50. The new proposal to sell the extra food won on a vote of 155 to 45. Even though some non-redheads voted with you and your fellow redheads, a large majority has now passed a law which causes redheads to suffer for no good reason. As a member of a permanent minority—20 redheads in a group of 200—your position in life is endangered by the principle of majority rule. Yet, you have no desire to establish a separate society for redheads only.

There are many permanent noticeable minorities in the 200 million-plus population of the United States. Are these minorities at the mercy of the will of the majority in the same way as the twenty redheads?

Minority Rights In any democratic society there is a tension between majority rule and minority rights. Minority rights are those protections and freedoms which the majority cannot simply vote to take away from individuals or minority groups. The basic definition of minority rights in the United States is in the Declaration of Independence. Jefferson wrote that all men and women have **inalienable** rights, including the right to life, liberty, and the pursuit of happiness.

The rights of minorities are carefully spelled out by the Constitution in the Bill of Rights and in other amendments. Decisions by the Supreme Court have interpreted the exact meanings of clauses about minority rights which were written into the Constitution. In the twentieth century, the Supreme Court has guarded and expanded the rights of minorities in the United States.

Exactly what are the rights of minorities? Freedom of speech, freedom of press, freedom of assembly are rights which no government—local, state, or federal—may take away from any citizen. These rights are especially important to minority groups. It is by using these methods of communication that a minority may persuade the majority to agree with a position. If a law hurts the interests of a group or if a law is needed to protect the interests of a group, that group must convince others of the need to do away with the harmful law or pass the needed law. Minorities convince others by making speeches, writing articles, holding meetings, and using radio and television. If members of the public never had an opportunity to see, hear, or read minority positions on important issues, changes and improvements in our society would seldom take place.

inalienable (in-AY-lee-un-uh-bl) An inalienable right is one which no government can take away.

The Chinese Exclusion Act of 1882 was an example of a law that hurt a minority. It denied citizenship to Chinese born in China and it remained in effect until World War II.

The Right to Education   At one time there were no public junior or senior high schools in the United States. A few citizens became convinced that secondary education as well as elementary education should be supported by public tax funds. This minority worked hard by using speeches, articles, and meetings to convince others of the advantage of having public high schools. If the majority, who at first opposed public high schools, had been able to stifle the minorities' right to freedom of speech, press, and assembly, their views in favor of public high schools could never have been accepted. Gradually, communities became convinced of the usefulness of public secondary education. Today, public support of education goes from kindergarten through twelfth grade, and in some states through college. Constructive changes of this type, first advocated by vocal minorities, make it possible for a democratic society to continue to exist and improve.

The Right to Religious Freedom   Another minority right is freedom of religion. No government—local, state, or federal—may support a particular religious denomination. No person may be discriminated against in politics, employment, housing, public accommodations, or

This drawing shows the Mormons on the westward trek through Illinois. The Supreme Court ruled that their religious practice of having more than one wife was illegal.

in any other manner because of that person's religious beliefs. One reason for freedom of religion is to prevent civil conflicts and even violence. Religious beliefs are deep ones. In a society such as the United States, if the government favored one denomination over others, conflicts would arise. Likewise, if religious discrimination were not forbidden, members of religious minorities would be at a disadvantage in obtaining political office, jobs, places to live, and other benefits controlled by members of large groups.

In the United States, church and state are separate. A basic problem that has arisen is how to determine what separate means. One place where this problem is most difficult to solve is in schools. Many cases have been brought before the Supreme Court by members of religious minorities who feel that their freedom of religion is being limited by the legal requirement that their children attend public school or by some of the religious activities conducted in public schools. Within recent years, the Supreme Court has banned Bible reading and prayer as routine parts of a public school's daily exercises. The purpose of the Court in making these rulings has generally been to separate church and state. Study of the Bible as a religious document or study of information about particular religions has not been banned. Since schools are a part of the state, the Supreme Court has tried to keep religious exercises out of schools in order to keep the state from lending even indirect support to a set of religious beliefs. Another purpose of the Court in banning Bible reading and prayer has been to protect minority religions and those who have no religious beliefs who must send their children to public schools in communities where the majority of citizens hold the same religious beliefs.

Property Rights   Another minority right is the right to have one's property protected from a government which is acting in the interests of a majority. This right protects "redheads" and other visible minorities from having their property taken or their access to the necessities of life limited by discriminatory laws.

Three parts of the Constitution have been used by the Supreme Court to protect the property rights of individuals and minorities. The Constitution has a clause that prevents governments from passing laws releasing persons from contractual obligations. If the majority of people in a town are in debt to the town banker, the town council cannot pass a law releasing those citizens from their debts. The Constitution also requires a government to make fair compensation when it takes over a piece of private property. This is especially important in cases where governments must get land upon which to build public buildings or roads. Although governments have the right to acquire property from an individual, no town government could force someone to accept a $100 payment for a lot on which the town wanted to build a school if the lot was worth $1,000. Citizens have a right to fair compensation when a government acquires their property.

The Right to Due Process   The Constitution also requires that no person be deprived of rights without due process of law. This means that if you are going to be fined for a criminal act, you must first be given a fair trial and proven guilty of the act. It also means that laws that are unfair will be declared unconstitutional. Any law restricting redheads to two meals a day would be declared unconstitutional. Even if the government can deprive you of property or freedom in the "public interest," it still must use a fair process to accomplish its purpose. For example, school principals cannot suspend unruly pupils from school for long periods of time without holding a due process hearing. This hearing would determine in a fair manner whether or not the accused student is guilty of misbehavior that deserves long-term suspension. In the cases where the Supreme Court extended the requirement for a due process hearing, the suspended student's right to an education—part of which is lost because of suspension—was treated as a property right.

The Limits of Minority Rights   None of the minority rights described so far are absolute rights. Each of these rights can be regulated, but not abolished or reduced, by government action. No one may exercise freedom of speech or press by telling untruths that damage another person's reputation. It is a violation of law to make a speech in a public place that incites a crowd to riot. At a public gathering it is illegal to suggest the use of violence to attack the government. Freedom of religion has been determined by the Supreme Court to mean freedom to believe almost anything. The Court has determined that governments may limit religious practices. Adult members of religious sects who force their children into dangerous practices such as handling poisonous snakes may be restrained by the government. Governments may limit the freedoms of some citizens to protect the majority of citizens in other ways. A government may impose quarantines where a person has a dangerous illness or cut down diseased trees of a homeowner if they threaten to destroy the rest of the trees in a community.

Establishing Minority Rights   How do we decide whether or not the will of the majority or the best interests of society will overcome the rights of a minority or an individual? The first battle is in the legislature. Any represented minority will argue against any proposed law which will damage its interests. If the law is passed anyway, the second battle is in the courts. Individuals and groups can and do bring suit in state and federal courts charging that laws or the manner in which laws are enforced are in violation of rights guaranteed in the Constitution. When judges decide such cases, they have to try to establish a delicate and fair balance between the rule of the majority and minority rights.

Native Americans have been subjected to unfair rulings by the majority. Pictured is tribal leader Nick Sapiel, whose tribe went to court over land in Maine.

SECTION CHECKUP

1. What does majority rule mean?
2. What are three rights guaranteed to minorities according to the Constitution?
3. What process is used by the government to obtain the property of an individual for governmental use when the individual does not wish to sell the property? How are the individual's rights protected?
4. What are three limits of minority rights?

4. EQUAL PROTECTION

Racial justice and equal protection under the law are topics which are woven together like threads in a piece of cloth. Many scholars of American government agree that one of our government's greatest failures throughout history has been its inability to promote the toleration of racial differences. The Civil War ultimately kept the nation united and freed the slaves, but a lot of hatred remained.

After the Civil War, the so-called reconstruction Amendments (Thirteenth, Fourteenth, and Fifteenth) established an exact definition of citizenship. The purpose of this was to protect freed Blacks from re-enslavement in fact, if not by law. The Fourteenth Amendment states: "No state shall...deny to any person within its jurisdiction the equal protection of the laws." What exactly does that mean? It means that state legislatures and Congress must not pass laws that allow certain groups of people to be disadvantaged by government. The government should give advantages to all. If legislatures were to pass laws forbidding all redheads to vote, or to work for the government, or to marry, these laws would be declared unconstitutional by the Supreme Court because they violate the equal protection clause of the Fourteenth Amendment. However, legislatures can pass laws requiring all persons to be eighteen years of age before voting, or requiring all persons who own property to pay taxes, or requiring all who marry to secure a license. All legislatures have to be able to make distinctions between persons and groups of persons in order to make laws. To understand the meaning of "equal protection," you must understand what types of distinctions are permitted and what types of distinctions are forbidden.

Classification of Minorities   In general, reasonable distinctions are permitted; age classification as it relates to the ability to vote is permitted. Unreasonable classifications are forbidden. If there is no connection between a permitted goal of the government and the establishment of a class of citizens, then the classification is not reasonable.

American society is exploring whether or not sex is a reasonable category. Shall we continue to permit legislatures to refer to certain bills as applicable only to women? An example of this is sick leave benefits for childbirth. Do laws such as this deny men the right to equal protection?

The Supreme Court automatically suspects certain types of classifications of groups and persons and usually forbids them. If a law is directed at a **suspect category,** the Supreme Court will examine it carefully. **Suspect categories** include race, religion, and national origin. A law making it more difficult for members of certain races or religions

The National Women's Conference, held in Texas, discussed issues involving the
Equal Rights Amendment. Do you recognize any of these people?

to vote would be declared unconstitutional. A law establishing a special tax to be paid only by citizens who were not born in the United States would be found unconstitutional.

The Supreme Court will also carefully look at state or federal laws dealing with the fundamental rights of persons, whether or not the laws define "suspect" categories. Rights are declared to be fundamental if they are implicitly or explicitly declared in the Constitution. All First Amendment rights plus the right to vote and the right to travel are considered fundamental. Rights that have not been declared fundamental, but which might be so declared in the future, include the right to an education, right to housing, or a right to receive welfare benefits.

Racial Justice The pursuit of racial justice in the United States during the twentieth century has many centers of interest. One of these

 ON CAREERS

Social Worker

A social worker is a person who helps others. When working with individuals, families, and groups, the social worker helps people solve their problems and get along better with other people around them. A social worker also works to provide, expand, improve, and create the social services available to individuals and communities. These social services may be recreation, health, education, or employment services. As our communities become larger it becomes more difficult for people to find the services they need. Therefore, the social worker is there to connect people with the appropriate services and programs.

Becoming a social worker requires at least four years of college. Two additional years of graduate school are necessary to become a professional social worker. If you have a keen interest in people and the confidence that people can overcome their problems with professional help, then social work can be a very satisfying career.

Miriam Birnbaum, a social worker at a community mental health center in New Rochelle, New York, has worked with neighborhood communities, the aged, the handicapped, the mentally retarded, and the emotionally disturbed. She has also taught and trained social work students at universities and in real situations. One day, Mrs. Birnbaum received a phone call from a woman who had been paralyzed by a stroke. She wanted to know of any programs that might be available to get her involved in activities outside her home. After making some inquiries, Mrs. Birnbaum found there were no such services available for stroke victims, so she decided to create some. As a result, there are now various recreational and social programs available for stroke-disabled adults in her area. Many other areas are now adopting such programs for their citizens, too.

interest areas has been the struggle to insure equal voting rights to members of all races. If a state government passes a law designed to prevent members of a certain race from exercising the right to vote, this would be an obvious denial of equal protection. This is true because the law depends on a suspect category (race) and because the law concerns a fundamental right (voting). No legislature would attempt to pass such a law at this time. However, toward the end of Reconstruction, the federal government lost interest in protecting the civil rights of freed slaves. At that time, Southern legislatures passed laws designed to make it hard for Black citizens to exercise their voting rights. Two types of laws were passed. Poll taxes required the payment of a sum of money before a person could register to vote. The amount of the tax was fixed to discourage Blacks and poor Whites from voting. Also, literacy tests were made a condition of registering to vote. Citizens desiring to register were forced to prove that they were able to read, write, and understand the Constitution by passing a test. In many cases, White registrars were prepared to certify all Whites as having passed the test while failing all Blacks.

Literacy tests and other obstacles to voting were often administered in an obviously prejudiced manner to prevent Blacks from voting in local, state, and national elections. The United States Commission on Civil Rights has documented many instances of counties and parishes in the United States excluding virtually all Black votes while still allowing illiterate Whites to vote. In the 1890s some state legislatures came to represent Whites only and passed the body of segregation laws known as "Jim Crow" laws.

The civil rights movement of the 1950s and 1960s had its beginning in the 1940s when lawyers of the National Association for the Advancement of Colored People (NAACP) succeeded in bringing cases to the Supreme Court that challenged the constitutionality of poll taxes, literacy tests, and other laws which violated equal protection in the area of voting. When the case-by-case method used by courts was unable to restore voting rights to Blacks and other minority races, the Congress of the United States began to pass laws designed to protect voting rights. The Civil Rights Acts of 1955, 1960, and 1964 all contained provisions designed to strengthen the ability of courts to act to protect the voting rights of minority groups. Finally, in the Voting Rights Act of 1965 and its 1970 amendments, the Congress took direct action with the purpose of guaranteeing all citizens the right to vote. This act provided for federal, rather than local, registration of voters in areas that had a long history of denying access to the polls to members of minority races. Using federal registrars and the threat of punishment for violations of the Voting Rights Act, Congress was able to achieve its purpose of guaranteeing equal protection of the law in the area of voting rights. All of the voting laws passed by Congress rested upon Section 5 of the Fourteenth Amendment. That section declares that Congress shall have the power to enforce all the other provisions of the Fourteenth Amendment, including the guarantee of equal protection of the law.

In a community where prejudice exists, its expression by government officials, law enforcement officers, jurors, and witnesses can unfairly slant the criminal justice process in favor of the majority race. In the twentieth century, the Supreme Court has issued many rulings on cases where defendants who were members of minority races have been unfairly treated by police officers, court officials, or juries. The

ONE STEP BEYOND—VOTING

The right to vote is an important guarantee of the Constitution as well as a major responsibility of all citizens. It is through this role that we determine the direction we wish our government to follow. Not all persons can vote. For example, an insane person cannot vote. A person who has been convicted of a felony is also ineligible. In some states, people who cannot read and write cannot vote. Specific requirements for voting are set by each state. They include the following:

1. A person must be a citizen of the United States.
2. The voter must be at least 18 years of age.
3. A person must have lived in the state a certain length of time. Depending upon the state, it may be as little as thirty days.
4. The voter must register to vote before the election. There is a specified date in each state which determines how many days before an election that registration must have been completed. When a person goes to register, that person's name, address, and age are given to the registrar. Before a person goes into the voting booth, the election official makes sure that the voter is properly registered. Each state allows persons to vote by absentee ballot. Many students and armed forces personnel follow this procedure when they are away from home on election day. They may secure an absentee ballot by writing to their local election board. Those persons must be registered before a ballot will be sent to them. Most states require that the absentee ballot be **notarized** or witnessed. This may be done by asking a notary public to certify the signature of the vote.

apprehension and trial of criminals is a matter left mostly to local governments. Therefore, the Supreme Court and the federal executive branch have had some difficulty in insuring that local justice would be color blind. Progress has been made. Many criminal convictions have been reversed when attorneys for the convicted persons have argued before the Supreme Court that equal protection of the law had been denied to their clients. As a result, many local officials have become more careful in giving equal protection to all persons.

The jury selection process has been a central point of concentration in the struggle for equal protection in the administration of justice. Until recently, many communities had a long history of excluding minorities from juries. Blacks and other racial minorities were often tried by juries from which minority group members had been excluded. This could be done by drawing jurors from the list of registered voters in a community which used poll taxes and literacy tests to keep minority group members from being able to register. To prevent injustice due to unfair jury selection procedures, the Supreme Court has ruled that race must not be considered when selecting a jury. Blacks cannot be excluded, because this is a denial of equal protection. However, there is no requirement that Blacks and other minorities be included.

Social Discrimination The effects of racial prejudice are felt in areas other than voting and the criminal justice system. In the past, members of minority groups have been denied equal access to homes, jobs, and public places such as restaurants and hotels or motels. In recent years, the Supreme Court has used the Fourteenth Amendment's guarantee of equal protection to declare unconstitutional laws which require any government official to act in a discriminatory manner against members of minority groups peacefully seeking their basic constitutional rights. If your private property is a restaurant, you cannot expect the police to help you enforce your refusal to serve Blacks or Native Americans. However, you can expect the police to help you enforce the health code regulation which forbids barefoot people to enter. Being barefoot is a reasonable category to be established by law.

What about strictly private acts of social discrimination? Are they legal? Can the Congress pass a law making private, non-state supported, discriminatory practices unlawful? The answer is yes. Congress first passed such a law shortly after the Civil War. The Civil Rights Act of 1866 states that "All citizens of the United States shall have the same right, in every state and territory, as is enjoyed by white citizens thereof to inherit, purchase, lease, sell, hold, and convey real and personal property." The Supreme Court has ruled that the Thirteenth Amendment gave Congress the authority to pass such laws. In the case of *Jones* v. *Mayer Co.* (1968) the Court ruled that the Mayer Company could not refuse to sell a house to Mr. and Mrs. Jones because they were Black. Even though no state action was involved in enforcing the refusal, the Supreme Court ruled that the Mayer Company could not violate the Jones's constitutional rights. In the same year (1968), the Congress dealt with discrimination in the sale and rental of housing. Real estate companies still have ways of discriminating when selling or renting housing.

A section of the Civil Rights Act of 1968 covers about 80 percent of the housing available in the country and forbids anyone to refuse to sell or rent the housing covered by the act on the basis of race, color, religion, or national origin. The power of Congress to pass such a law rests ultimately upon the Thirteenth and Fourteenth Amendments. Since 1968, the Supreme Court has upheld the Civil Rights Acts of 1866 and 1968. There is now no doubt that Congress has the power to pass any legislation it sees fit in order to insure that no citizens will

NEGRO EXPULSION FROM RAILWAY CAR, PHILADELPHIA.

Blacks were often forced out of railroad cars if they did not sit in segregated sections of the train.

suffer discriminatory practices because of their race. This power applies whether the discrimination is a form of state action or is a private action. Racial discrimination in all its forms can be made illegal.

Fair treatment of all citizens in the society was an ideal goal of those who founded our government. Equal protection of the law is the constitutional requirement applied to all citizens. Because the country did not live up to the ideal of fairness represented by equal protection, a long struggle to guarantee civil rights to racial minorities has taken place. Equal protection has been used in that struggle to insure that no law be passed to reserve benefits to members of the White majority.

Equal protection is usually concerned with the standard of fairness found in the law itself. Laws cannot weaken access to fundamental rights nor be directed at "suspect" categories such as races. The struggle for fairness has another part, which is the question of whether or not laws are fairly enforced and administered. Just as the right to equal protection insures the fairness of the law itself, so the right to what is called due process insures to each individual that laws will be enforced and administered fairly.

CASE STUDY

A Black couple applied for an apartment in a very rich section of a town. The wife was a chemist. The husband was a medical doctor. They were told that there were no vacancies. Two days later, a White couple applied at the same building. The husband was unemployed. The wife was a teacher. They got an apartment. Would you say that the Black family was discriminated against? Why?

SECTION checkup

1. What does equal protection mean?
2. Which two of the amendments to the Constitution are most directly related to providing equal protection for all citizens?
3. What were the two types of laws passed during the Reconstruction period that denied equal opportunity in voting?
4. What is the name of the organization that has done most to gain equal rights for Black people?

CHAPTER REVIEW

American citizens value the basic freedoms as listed in the Bill of Rights. One of these—freedom of speech—is almost an absolute right. The Supreme Court prohibits prior restraint on the freedom of people to speak their opinions in public. Although the government can be criticized in public, slander is illegal. Statements that pose a "clear and present" danger of causing harm to others can be restrained. Our democratic political processes, as well as every individual's need to be completely informed about what is happening in the world, depend upon freedom of speech.

The minorities in this country have been discriminated against throughout our history. There has been a gradual trend to solve many of the problems suffered by minorities and at the same time maintain the stability of a democratic society. In recent years, laws have been passed which clarified many of the provisions in the Constitution and the Bill of Rights that related to the guaranteed rights of minorities.

In addition, the Supreme Court has ruled on many cases related to equal rights of minorities. Their decisions have had far-reaching results in our society.

QUESTIONS FOR REVIEW

1. Describe how at least three minorities have experienced less-than-equal protection under the law.
2. Describe actions taken by the federal government in the last thirty years that have changed the rights of minorities.
3. What other First Amendment freedoms help American citizens maintain a democratic society in much the same way that freedom of speech helps citizens maintain a democracy?
4. What First Amendment freedoms are more absolute than freedom of speech? Less absolute than freedom of speech?
5. What is the difference between majority and minority rights?
6. How are minority rights established?

1. Each of you is a member of a minority group in some way. Identify that minority and write a brief description of how you feel about this aspect of your life.
2. Interview a person from another ethnic group. Write a brief description of how that person's life differs from your own.
3. Make a list of the criticisms of government that you have heard expressed on television. Decide whether or not you agree with the criticisms on your list.
4. Write a letter to the editor of the newspaper you read which expresses your views on a controversial subject such as the ERA.
5. Create an example of the type of speech that you think should be restrained. Ask your teacher and classmates to determine whether or not it would be constitutional for your local government to pass a law restraining speeches of this type.
6. Check the newspaper (either current or back issues) for items dealing with court cases arising from government confiscation of private property for governmental use. Write a history of the case.
7. Divide the class into three groups. Each member will (a) interview a minister of any religion of his or her choice and obtain an interpretation of the First Amendment in regard to freedom of religion, or (b) interview an attorney about decisions made by the Supreme Court in regard to freedom of religion.

YOUR LAW LIBRARY

Haiman, Franklyn S., *Freedom of Speech.* Skokie, Illinois: National Textbook, 1976.

Konvitz, Milton R., *Bill of Rights Reader.* Ithaca, N.Y.: Cornell University Press, 1973.

Lathan, Frank B., *American Justice on Trial.* New York: Franklin Watts, 1972.

McDonald, Laughlin, *Racial Equality.* Skokie, Illinois: National Textbook, 1977.

Pfeller, Leo, *Religious Freedom.* Skokie, Illinois: National Textbook, 1977.

CRIMINAL LAW AND YOUR RIGHTS

chapter
4

Every community in the world has some criminals. The United States is no exception. Unlike many nations, however, we not only try to protect ourselves from criminal acts but also from wrongful arrest and imprisonment by the very forces we have set up to protect us. We have a Constitution which guarantees certain rights to a person accused of a crime. Furthermore, a specific process has been set up to deal with crime. This process must be followed every time a person is accused of a crime. Someone accused of a crime is told of these rights and this process when arrested. During the trial the person is informed again by the lawyer who defends him or her.

There are many types of crimes. With thousands of people involved in each of them, you might even say they have become a big business. These crimes are committed not only by adults. At least one half of all crimes in the United States are committed by young people. Many people believe that crime can be lessened if young people are carefully educated about their rights and about the seriousness of following a life of crime. If young people see the value of a crimeless society then we might expect to improve our relationships with each other. As a final result, we might improve our whole way of life.

OBJECTIVES

To know the basic philosophy of the Constitution as it relates to persons accused of crimes.

To be able to list the major types of crimes and to give an example of each one.

To be able to list in their correct order the steps of the criminal process.

To be able to describe the process of dealing with juvenile offenders and to compare it with the process of dealing with the adult criminals.

1. THE GUARANTEED RIGHTS OF A PERSON ACCUSED OF A CRIME

The founders of our nation were wise when they constructed the Constitution of the United States. Aware of the lack of personal freedom in other countries, they were careful to see that citizens of this young country would have some guaranteed rights. It was important, they felt, that those persons accused of criminal acts be safe from **undue persecution.**

The basic idea of the Constitution on this matter is that every person is considered innocent until proven guilty.

The Fourth Amendment The Fourth, Fifth, Sixth, and Eighth Amendments to the United States Constitution deal with these rights. The Fourth Amendment states that people have a right to be secure in their person, their homes, papers, and **effects** against unreasonable search and seizures. For a search or seizure to be lawful, a **warrant** must be obtained from a judge. The judge must agree that there is ample proof of the need for the search or seizure. A warrant is a written authorization of a judge or **magistrate** to arrest a specific person or search a specific place. The warrant must describe the place to be searched and the persons or things to be seized.

The Supreme Court has placed the following areas within the protection of the Fourth Amendment: a business office, a store, a car, a hotel room, an apartment, a taxi. Lower courts have added hospital rooms, school lockers, and an employee's unlocked desk to the list of protected areas.

The Fifth Amendment The Fifth Amendment guarantees that a person cannot be made to answer to a capital crime (crime punishable by death) such as murder unless that person is **indicted** by a grand jury. An indictment is a formal accusation of a crime made against a person. It is made by a grand jury upon the repuest of a **prosecutor.** In some states, a magistrate can make the indictment. This insures that the case against the person is known by a person or persons other than

Undue persecution (un-DOO per-suh-KEW-shun) means to pursue, or harass someone excessively for a supposed criminal act.

Effects (eh-FEX) are things belonging to a person, such as clothes, jewelry, etc.

A **warrant** (WAR-unt) is a legal document that permits a police officer to search a place.

A **magistrate** (MA-jus-trate) is an officer charged with administering the laws.

A **prosecutor** (PRAH-suh-kew-ter) is an official who begins and carries out proceedings in a court of law.

1. Must have a speedy trial.
2. Right to have a trial by an impartial jury of the state and district wherein the crime was committed.
3. Right to have a qualified defense attorney.
4. May not be forced to testify or be a witness against oneself.
5. Witnesses must appear in one's behalf.
6. Right to confront all accusers.
7. Right to have accusers cross-examined by the defense attorney.
8. May not be tried twice for the same crime (double jeopardy).
9. Right to due process of law.
10. Excessive bail is not to be imposed.
11. Rights against unreasonable search and seizure.

the arresting officer. This amendment also states that a person cannot be tried twice for the same crime **(double jeopardy).** Also, a person cannot be forced to testify against himself or herself in a criminal case. This part of the Constitution is used often by many persons involved in criminal procedures. They state in court that they "refuse to testify on grounds that it may tend to incriminate them." Lastly, this amendment states that a citizen shall not be deprived of life, liberty, or property, without **due process of law.** By due process a citizen knows that all steps in the process that are required by law must be followed before the case is decided.

The Sixth Amendment The Sixth Amendment states that an "accused person shall enjoy the right to a speedy and public trial, by an **impartial** (or unbiased) jury of the state and district" in which the crime was committed. The accused is to be told of the nature and cause of the accusation and to face witnesses against him or her. Witnesses for the accused must be obtained. The accused also has the right to a defense attorney.

Even though these rights are clearly stated, there are often long delays in the final criminal process. The right to a speedy trial relates to when a trial begins, not when it ends. A trial can often last several months. If the accused person in a long trial is poor, he or she often cannot raise **bail** and so may have to spend several months in jail. **Bail** allows an

As a result of a biased community, Nicola Sacco and Bartolemeo Vanzetti were executed in 1927 for armed robbery and murder even though there was no direct evidence linking them to the crime.

accused person to be released from custody during the period between arrest and the final judgment of the case. This process often requires that the person put up a specified amount of money or property, which will be turned over to the court if the person fails to come to trial. At the end of the trial that person could be found innocent.

Currently, many courts in our judicial system are so overwhelmed with criminal cases that it is impossible to try all the cases as quickly as the founders of our nation expected. At times, it is the defendant who asks that the trial be postponed. He or she may have nothing to lose and much to gain in witnesses dying, or moving, or losing memory of the incident.

The Eighth Amendment   The Eighth Amendment states that "excessive bail shall not be required, nor excessive fines imposed, nor cruel and unusual punishments inflicted."

Due Process   The term **due process** occurs twice in the amendments to the Constitution. It is first used in the Fifth Amendment, which prohibits Congress from depriving a person of life, liberty, or property without due process of law. It applies to actions of the federal

The United States Supreme Court in the **Miranda** v. **Arizona** case said that all questioning while an individual is in custody is **coercive** and certain warnings are needed to reduce the coercive atmosphere. Therefore, the court ruled that before any questioning, the person must be told of his or her right to remain silent. That person must be told that any statement made can be used as evidence at a later date. The defendant must also be advised that he or she has a right to an attorney. If the individual is unable to pay for counsel, an attorney will be appointed. The accused may **waive** or refuse, these rights, if the waiver is made voluntarily, knowingly, and intelligently. Even if the defendant has answered some questions, the right to refrain from answering any more questions until an attorney has been consulted is guaranteed.

The decision in this case has led to the requirement that police officers must advise persons being arrested of their guaranteed rights to remain silent and to get the advice of counsel before being questioned.

---

government. It is not known exactly what those who wrote the Constitution had in mind when they used the term.

The term was used again in the Fourteenth Amendment. It said that no state shall deprive any person of life, liberty, or property, without due process of law. Note that **state** is included in the phrase in this amendment. This amendment was passed to insure that all persons regardless of race or color would be given due process of law.

Criminal Prosecution   Up until 1927, it was understood that a criminal prosecution in the courts of a state which was conducted in accordance with the law of the state was **due process** in the constitutional sense. At that time, the United States Supreme Court ruled on a case. It stated that the accused had not been given due process because the procedure used by the state court was unfair.

Consistent Treatment   In 1943 the United States Supreme Court decided what "fair" or "unfair" meant. It declared that to be fair all that was required was that state procedures agree with the basic ideas of liberty and justice. Recently the court has interpreted due process more strictly. It has set requirements upon state procedure which are not rooted in tradition nor related to basic principles.

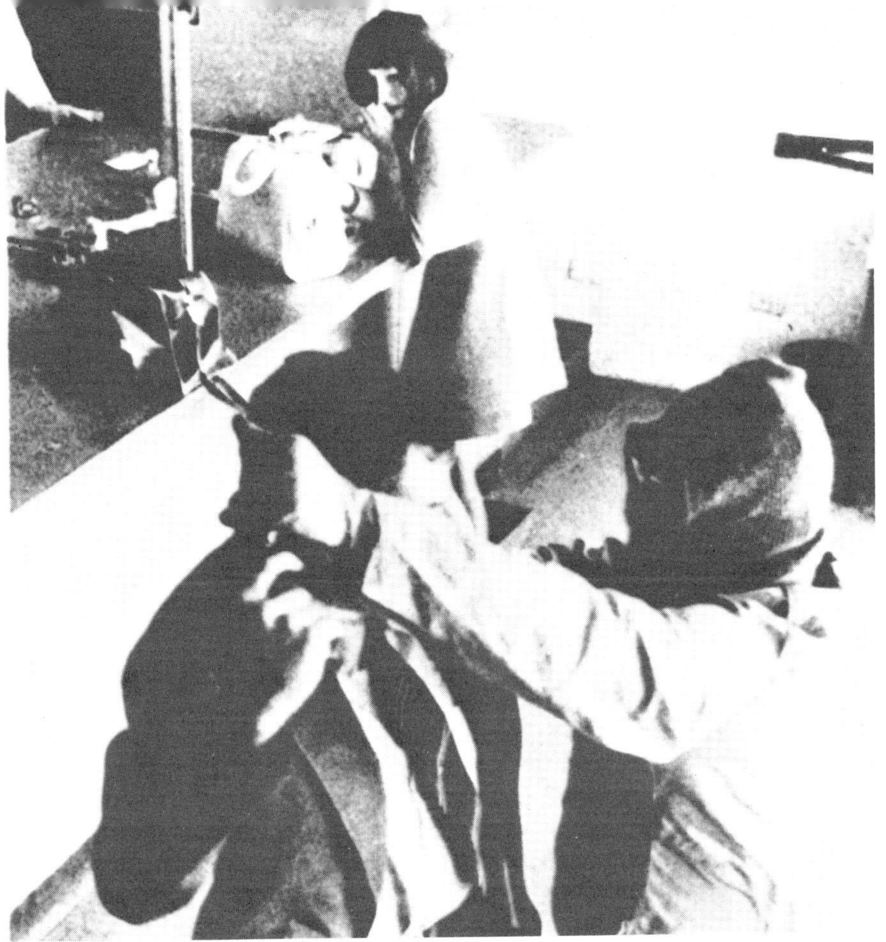

A hidden camera captured this bank robbery scene. What type of crime is armed robbery?

Modern Interpretation   Today, criminal procedure in each state operates within two constitutional frameworks. The first is made up of the limitations contained in the state's constitution. The second is the federal requirements of **due process of law.** This requirement is interpreted by the United States Supreme Court as it rules on cases presented to it. The exact meaning of **due process** is unclear. It means what the Supreme Court of the United States says it means at any one particular time.

SECTION CHECKUP

1. What are the four amendments to the United States Constitution that deal with the criminal process?
2. Define **double jeopardy.**
3. List each of the eleven guaranteed rights of an accused person.
4. What are the two constitutional frameworks that the criminal procedure operates on today?

2. CRIME IN THE UNITED STATES

Crimes are grouped as infractions, misdemeanors, and felonies. An **infraction** is a minor offense that carries no moral **stigma** and is punishable by a fine. A good example of an infraction is a parking violation. A **misdemeanor** is a crime punishable by a fine, by imprisonment in a county jail, or by both. Some common misdemeanors are speeding, disorderly conduct, and trespassing.

A **felony** is a serious crime that is punishable by imprisonment in a state prison for a year or longer. In some instances a felony is punishable by death. Laws may state that some crimes such as murder are felonies. When the law requires that a person be placed in a state prison, the crime is considered a felony.

A person convicted of a felony usually suffers **suspension** of all civil political rights, such as the right to vote. If sentenced to life in prison, that person loses his or her civil political rights permanently. This involves the right to vote and hold political office as well as other political rights. Losing one's civil rights does not mean losing constitutional rights. The rights guaranteed in the Constitution such as freedom of speech, religion, and so on are kept. In the event that a person is given a suspended sentence and put on **probation,** that person automatically has the right to vote again when the period of probation is over. Many professionals such as physicians, attorneys, pharmacists, and dentists lose their licenses if they are convicted of a felony.

Criminal Intent   Almost all crimes require a **criminal intent.** This means that a person must mean or intend to commit a crime. This does not mean **motive,** however. The motive is the need or desire that causes a person to commit the crime. When prosecuting the case, the prosecutor need not prove that a motive exists. A good motive can never justify a criminal act. Robin Hood had a good motive for his actions. He robbed the rich to give to the poor but his actions were still unlawful.

A charge of criminal negligence is based on the idea that a crime may be committed through careless or reckless action. For example, parents who allow their child to drive the family car without giving proper driving instructions are guilty of criminal negligence if their child causes an accident. **Regulatory offenses** are treated in much the same way. An example of a regulatory offense is breaking a state or federal law that involves the quality of food sold to others. Even though there may have been no criminal intent, the person who broke the law is guilty of a criminal act.

Crime Against a Person   Some of the most common types of crimes are those committed against a person, property, public health, safety and welfare, and public decency and morals.

Crime against a person involves such acts as murder, manslaughter, extortion, assault and battery, and kidnapping. Murder means the unlawful killing of a human being with **malice aforethought.** When a person murders another after thinking it through, it is considered first-degree murder. When murder is committed as a result of an unjustified rage, it is classified as second-degree murder. First-degree murder is punishable by life imprisonment and, in some states, by death. Second-degree murder usually results in imprisonment from five years to life.

Murders   The greater number of murders are committed by family members, relatives, or friends of the victims. Therefore, there is some truth to the statement that if you are afraid of being murdered, you will be safer if you leave your family and friends than if you depend on additional police protection. This is because the police rarely have the chance to keep friends and relatives from murdering one another.

Manslaughter   Manslaughter is the unlawful killing of another without malice aforethought. Manslaughter is classified in two different ways. Generally, manslaughter during the heat of passion is called **voluntary** and manslaughter through accidental conduct is **involuntary.**

Malice aforethought (MA-luss uh-FOUR-thawt) means that someone who has committed a crime made specific plans to commit it.

CASE STUDY

Consider this case. Three children were left at home unattended while their parents were working in a field nearby. One child, a ten-year-old boy, became angry at his eleven-year-old brother. He went to the rack where his father's shotgun was kept and then found some shells in a drawer. He loaded the gun and shot his brother. The child admitted the incident to the sheriff. Due to his age, the youngster was not prosecuted. However, the parents of the boy could possibly be prosecuted for negligence.

A woman became upset when a group of young boys began using part of her backyard as a testing ground for their minibikes. In order to stop them, she tied a rope between two trees across the path that was being used. The next morning two boys came by on a minibike. Being unaware of the rope, they ran into it. One of the boys was killed. Is the woman guilty of manslaughter? If so, of what type of manslaughter is she guilty? She could be prosecuted for involuntary manslaughter.

Extortion   This is another type of crime against a person. Extortion means getting money or property by threatening injury to a person or to his or her family. Extortion is often associated with **kidnapping—**

Charles and Anne Morrow Lindbergh were victims of extortion. Here, they arrive at the court for the trial of the man accused of kidnapping and murdering their son.

the unlawful seizure and secret **confinement** of a person without that person's consent.

The most famous case of kidnapping and extortion in American history involved the son of Charles and Anne Morrow Lindbergh. Lindbergh had gained fame and fortune by being the first man to fly across the Atlantic Ocean alone in his airplane, "The Spirit of St. Louis." Anne Morrow Lindbergh was the daughter of a famous American diplomat. Their infant son was kidnapped and murdered. The kidnapper extorted a large sum of money from the Lindberghs by promising to return their son. The kidnapper was caught and executed for the crime. As a result of this case Congress passed a law in 1932 which enables the Federal Bureau of Investigation to officially enter the investigation of any kidnapping twenty-four hours after it takes place. After that period of time, it is assumed that the victim has been taken from one state to another. So, the federal government may intervene under the Interstate Commerce Clause of the Constitution.

Assault and Battery   Two other types of crime **against the person** are **assault** and **battery.** An **assault** is an unlawful attempt to violently injure the person of another. The person responsible for an assault must also have the ability to injure. A **battery** is an unlawful injury to the person of another. Therefore, an assault is an attempt to commit a battery. An example of an assault would be for one person to attempt to strike another with a fist, but miss. Battery would be actually striking the person with a fist.

Crime against Property   Crime against property involves offenses such as burglary, robbery, theft, and arson. **Burglary** occurs when a person enters a residence (if its doors are locked) with intent to commit a crime. **Robbery** is the taking of property from another person by the use of force or by threat. Robbery is an offense against both property and person.

Theft is another crime against property. There are two varieties of theft. The first is **grand theft** and it is a felony. **Grand theft** is the stealing of personal property of great value. States vary as to the dollar value placed on theft before it is considered grand theft. Stealing a car is an example of grand theft. The other type is called **petty theft.** Shoplifting is generally regarded as petty theft depending on the value of the articles stolen.

Arson is also a crime against property. It involves the unlawful burning of a building or other personal property. Arson is often committed to obtain insurance money illegally. Some people commit arson just for a thrill. When a person sets a fire and another person is killed in the fire, the arsonist is charged with first-degree murder.

Crimes against Public Health, Safety, and Welfare   There are also crimes against public health, safety, and welfare. These crimes include such offenses as transporting a loaded gun in a motor vehicle, violating laws regulating food, drugs, liquor, and cosmetics, disobeying fish and game laws, and a host of other related violations.

Crimes against Public Decency and Morals   These crimes involve offenses against public decency and morals. This includes public drunkenness, drug abuse, illegal gambling, contributing to the delinquency of a minor, and other similar offenses.

Organized Crime   The American public has been aware of criminal gangs for many years. Gangland wars of the 1920s and '30s led to the much-publicized conviction of gangster Al Capone on income tax evasion. It seems that the law enforcement agencies could not find enough evidence for conviction on other crimes in which he may have been involved.

In the years that followed, organized crime operated mostly in secrecy. These secret organizations engaged in almost every conceivable type of criminal violence. Among them were murder, traffic in drugs, smuggling, extortion, kidnapping, and labor racketeering.

"The Sting" was the name given to an operation in Washington, D.C. by police to break up local **fencing** of stolen goods. The police set up a local business to receive property which had been stolen. They paid the thieves the going rate for the stolen goods. The police posed as mobsters under false names to gain the confidence of their clients.

They operated for several weeks under the name of P.F.F., Inc. which stood for Police, FBI, Fencing, Inc. They took in over $2.4 million worth of loot. Each transaction was photographed.

At the end of the operation, the police decided to throw a party for their "clients." About 100 persons, many dressed in tuxedoes, were arrested on the spot when they showed up for the party. Other "clients" who did not show up were arrested later. One of the men arrested was a self-styled "hit man" (a killer for hire). He gave the police a resumé of his experiences in hopes of getting a job with organized crime. At least 152 persons were arrested. Of this number, 105 were found to be free on parole or probation for a previous offense, or on some form of pretrial release, such as bail, on pending charges. In addition, 114 of them (or 70 percent) had prior criminal convictions.

Fencing means receiving and selling stolen goods.

Many movies of the 1930s portrayed the violence and criminal acts of organized crime. Do you recognize these characters?

Secrecy   Some of the secrecy of organized crime was stripped away in 1957. State police broke up a meeting of 75 or more crime bosses from all over the country in Appalachin, New York. None of the bosses would confess that a secret crime organization actually existed. However, enough evidence was disclosed in further investigations and in the trial to show that there was a nationwide system of crime.

The Profit of Crime   It is estimated that organized crime takes in about $40 billion each year. The chief sources are gambling, **loan sharking,** and narcotics. More recently, organized crime has taken over legitimate businesses.

ONE STEP BEYOND—CIGARETTE SMUGGLING

Many states have placed relatively high taxes on the sale of cigarettes. New York, for example, has a tax of about $2 per carton of cigarettes. These states see the cigarette tax as a good source of income. The yield, however, has not been as great as anticipated because of the cigarette smuggling.

The states of North and South Carolina, Virginia, and Kentucky both grow and manufacture tobacco products. Cigarette taxes in these states are very low. Organized crime is able to buy cigarettes in these states at low prices in large quantities, transport them to northern states to sell them at discount prices and still make a huge profit. This profit is due to the fact that no tax is paid to that state for the sale of cigarettes. The crime system, or **syndicate**, has managed to develop machines capable of making counterfeit tax stamps. So persons buying the cigarettes are usually unaware that they are buying an unlawful item. These people are unknowingly contributing to organized crime.

It is estimated that the states with high cigarette taxes are losing several hundred millions of dollars each year in unpaid taxes on cigarettes. These states have suggested that the problem lies with the "tobacco states." They feel that the tobacco states should raise their taxes to the same level as the taxes they charge. The tobacco states, on the other hand, are afraid that higher taxes will affect the sale of cigarettes and thereby harm the economy and industry of their states. What do you think the solution is?

SECTION Checkup

1. What is the difference between a **misdemeanor,** a **felony,** and an **infraction?**
2. What is the difference between **first-** and **second-degree** murder?
3. What does **extortion** mean?
4. What are the two types of **manslaughter,** and what does each mean?
5. Describe the extent of organized crime in this country and list some of its activities.

3. THE CRIMINAL PROCESS

Criminal procedure varies from state to state and from place to place. The type of crime involved also has an effect on the procedure. Let us look at the process normally followed in felony prosecutions in city courts.

Pre-arrest Investigation   When police are made aware of a crime, they investigate the situation to gather all available facts before they make an **arrest.** Arrest may be defined as the act of taking a person into custody. The most common types of investigation are observations at the scene of the crime and interviews with witnesses. Sometimes police use "tips" from informants and undercover agents. **Surveillance**—that is watching and/or following a suspect—is another method used.

Police power can be used only if there is clear justification for any power used by the police. Basically, the police may do the following:

1. Investigate where there are reasons to investigate.
2. Stop a citizen where there is a reason or where the citizen is acting in a suspicious manner.
3. **Frisk** the citizen when the officer's safety is felt to be in danger.
4. Hold and question the citizen where there is cause and necessity based on facts.
5. Arrest where there are sufficient facts to believe the citizen has committed a crime.
6. Search the location to protect the officer and to prevent the destruction of evidence.
7. Seize any evidence of the crime.

To **frisk** means to search someone rapidly.

Some crimes are committed with very poor planning. One such case was the robbery of a grocery store during the day by a person who was known by the clerk. The robber ran out of the door with the clerk chasing him. Another man was waiting in the getaway car. The clerk spotted a policeman in the parking lot and called for help. The robbers drove by the store twice trying to find a way out of the parking lot with the police chasing them. The chase continued out of town into a rural area where the robbers threw the money out of the car and sped away. They were finally caught. As they were being forced from the car, the police became aware that there was a third passenger in the car—a skunk!

In many cases, the police engage in some form of search. This may be the search of the person involved or of a vehicle or home. Police have no independent power to search. They can search when it is necessary to protect themselves in emergencies. Police may search when they have search warrants issued by the courts. Finally, police may search when the citizen consents to being searched. In most cases, the search is usually made with the consent of the suspect or is done at the same time as an arrest. Only in a small number of cases is a search warrant issued before the search.

When taking a person into lawful custody, police may search the arrested person for weapons, **contraband,** items used to commit the crime, as well as evidence connected with the crime. Searches made hours after the arrest are illegal and unreasonable. Under all circumstances, there is no right to search until an arrest has been made.

Contraband (KAHN-truh-band) is stolen goods.

The Arrest   The decision to make an arrest is made by the officer investigating the crime. An arrest can be made by an officer without a warrant, under the following conditions:

A police officer who misuses his or her arrest power may be sued for "false arrest" (TORT). The officer must then pay damages out of his or her own pocket.

1. When a crime is committed or attempted in his or her presence.
2. When the person arrested has committed a felony, even though not in the presence of the officer.
3. When a felony has been committed and the arresting officer has reasonable cause to believe it was committed by the person being arrested.

Newsmen and spectators are frisked before entering a courtroom. Why is frisking necessary?

However, in some cases, the officer is acting on a warrant issued by a local judge or magistrate. Generally, only 10 to 15 percent of all police encounters with suspects will result in an arrest. Because there are no set rules as to when and whom a police officer may arrest, the officer is left with a great deal of power to arrest people as he or she sees fit.

Being arrested can destroy the reputation of a citizen. A criminal record will follow people through all the days of their lives. Employment opportunities become very small for anyone who has been arrested.

Booking   After an arrest has been made, the suspect is taken to the police department. Shortly after arrival, the suspect is usually **booked.** Booking involves nothing more than entering the suspect's name, time of arrest, and the offense involved in the police department arrest book. The suspect may also be fingerprinted, photographed, and asked to submit a handwriting sample, depending on the seriousness of the crime.

ON CAREERS

Policewomen

Women are joining the ranks of law enforcement agencies in ever-increasing numbers. Until recent years, women were used only in specialized roles. They are currently being used in regular patrol work in many areas. This has been one of the results of the equal-rights-for-women movement. However, there is still wide disapproval of women being assigned to the same duties as men. Some men feel that some of the duties are too dangerous and strenuous for women to perform. At this point there is no evidence available that could be used either to support or deny the view that women on patrol duty perform as effectively as men. If the trend continues, there will be even more positions open for women in various areas of law enforcement.

Detective Lucille Burrascano, Crime Prevention Specialist, began her career with the police department as a police officer eight years ago. She now speaks all over New York City on building and personal safety. She also works with individuals, neighborhoods, and tenants. Detective Burrascano works with senior citizens and advises them how to safeguard themselves against crime.

When people wish to make their homes safe, they call Detective Burrascano. As she approaches their neighborhood, she makes note of shrubbery, poor street lighting, and areas where criminals might lurk. She also locates police call boxes. She studies the crime statistics of the police precinct of that particular area. Once she has surveyed the house, she then writes up a report and makes suggestions to the owner on how to improve security. This might mean replacing locks, installing an alarm system, or getting acquainted with the neighbors in case their help is needed.

Detective Burrascano has worked hard to achieve her detective's gold shield. She hopes to become a police commissioner.

Detention (dee-TEN-shun) means holding someone accused of a crime in a penal institution.

The Decision to Prosecute   A copy of the arresting officer's report is sent to the prosecutor. The prosecutor determines whether the person should be charged with the offense. If the prosecutor decides that there is a case against the suspect, a complaint is prepared which identifies and specifies the charge against that person. In some areas, the prosecutor must also get an arrest warrant from the court. This process leads to the continued **detention** of the defendant.

A policewoman, armed with a service revolver, is shown in action here.

The First Appearance—Presentment   Laws in most states require that an arrested person be taken before a local magistrate without a long delay. The magistrate informs the defendant of: (1) charges; (2) constitutional rights; (3) the right to a **preliminary hearing**; (4) the right to be represented by counsel (if the defendant is poor, many states provide an appointed counsel at this point); and (5) amount of bail.

The Preliminary Hearing   The purpose of the preliminary hearing is to protect a person from unjust prosecution. At the hearing, the prosecutor must produce enough evidence so that the magistrate believes that the defendant could have committed a felony. If the magistrate decides that there is enough evidence to have a trial, then the defendant stays in custody. Then the prosecutor must prepare the official charge against the defendant.

Grand Jury Indictment   Sometimes, the decision to prosecute must be approved by a grand jury, not in a preliminary hearing. The grand jury is composed of up to 23 private citizens who meet behind closed doors. They consider the evidence presented by the prosecutor. The defendant may not offer his or her own evidence or be present when the grand jury meets. If the grand jury decides that there is enough evidence for a trial, it will issue an **indictment.** The **indictment** is a written accusation, prepared by the prosecutor and signed by the grand jury. It charges the defendant with a specific crime.

The Prosecutor

The prosecutor or district attorney works for the government to proceed legally against a person accused of a crime. It is the job of the prosecutor or district attorney to represent the state or the people. "District" means that there is a specified territory that is within the district attorney's jurisdiction. That area is usually a county. The official title for the office may be county attorney or county prosecutor. In the federal system the title is United States attorney.

The prosecutor is elected in some states and appointed in others. The term of office is usually four years. The President appoints United States attorneys and they are responsible to the Attorney General.

Once a person is arrested, it is up to the prosecutor to determine whether or not there is enough evidence to actually have a case. If there is sufficient evidence, then he or she must decide what the formal charge will be.

Prosecutors also act as attorneys for the government in civil suits to take property for public use or to collect taxes. He or she may also defend the government in suits brought against it by people or groups.

Mr. Richard B. Lowe III is an assistant district attorney. He prepared for his career by attending college for four years and then going to law school. After finishing law school he passed the Bar Examination. He was then recruited from law school for his job as an assistant District Attorney.

Mr. Lowe spends long hours reviewing evidence in order to determine if a case is going to be tried in court. If he decides that the case is to be tried, he must appear in court with a defense attorney to select a jury. He also works closely with the police in a case. Many times he works after office hours in order to prepare his case. An assistant district attorney must have confidence in his case but must also be prepared to hand over any useful evidence to the defense which could result in the prosecutor losing the case.

Mr. Lowe indicated that many of the best defense attorneys were once prosecutors. However, unlike most defense attorneys, most prosecutors do not make large salaries. The training a prosecutor acquires is most valuable for future law-related work.

Arraignment   After the indictment is filed, the defendant is arraigned. The arraignment takes place in a trial court. The defendant is informed of the charges and the pleas that may be entered. The pleas are usually guilty, not guilty, **nolo contendere** or not guilty by reason of insanity. If the defendant is poor, counsel may be appointed at this point. If the defendant does not want counsel or already has counsel, the plea will usually be entered. Where the defendant refuses to plead, a plea of not guilty will ordinarily be entered.

Pretrial Motions   If the defendant pleads "not guilty," objections or motions are likely to be raised before the trial takes place. Some of the objections raised might include prior jeopardy (an earlier trial for the same offense), lack of enough evidence, the statute of limitation (too much time has passed since the crime was committed), or irregular procedure of the grand jury. The attorney can ask for dismissal based on objections such as these.

Nolo contendere means I do not wish to contend. It is a plea by the defendant that without admitting guilt subjects him or her to a judgment of conviction as in a plea of guilty but does not stop him or her from denying the truth of the charges.

ONE STEP BEYOND—PLEA BARGAINING

The most common method used to get rid of criminal cases in the American judicial system is **plea bargaining.** This action can take place at three different levels. They include the prosecuting attorney, the judge, and in some cases, the probation officer. The prosecuting attorney probably uses it most. The prosecutor must decide if there is ample evidence to prosecute and whether or not to bargain with the accused so that there will be a plea of guilty in exchange for a lesser charge with lighter penalty. The practice of encouraging offenders to plead guilty as a result of plea bargaining has been justified in several ways. First, crimes have increased in numbers. This results in an overload which the courts cannot handle and which places an increased burden on the public because of time needed for witnesses and additional juries. Second, the law may be considered too severe. Third, there may be **mitigating circumstances.** Fourth, the case for the state may not be strong enough to get a conviction. Finally, the public prosecutor is elevated according to the number of convictions he or she has obtained.

Mitigating circumstances (MII I-tuh-gayt-ing) are facts that do not justify or excuse an action, but which can lower the amount of blame and thus reduce the criminal punishment for an action.

Forensic Technician

It is the job of the **forensic team** to find clues to help the police solve a crime. They take charge at the scene of a homicide as soon as they arrive. They take photographs and fingerprints, and examine other physical evidence that can be found. For the team to be successful, it is necessary for everything at the scene of a homicide to be intact on its arrival. Police officers are asked not to touch anything or search for clues at the scene. There are things that the first police officer on the scene should be aware of. These might include ice cubes in a glass, water on the floor, or other types of evidence which might not be present when the forensic team arrives. When the team completes its investigation at the scene and in its laboratory, all evidence is turned over to the chief law enforcement official. Then that person is charged with the duty of solving the crime. In many cases, evidence the team finds leads to the conviction of a criminal.

Detective Arnold Roussine has been a forensic technician for 17 years. He was previously a police officer and had a knowledge of photography and science. He received forensic investigative training from that unit of the police department.

During a typical day, Detective Roussine and his partner may be notified of a murder. When they arrive at the scene of the crime, it has been sealed off to the public by the police to insure that nothing has been touched or disturbed since the crime was committed. First, Detective Roussine photographs the entire area. Then he and his partner process the area and victim for fingerprints. They do this by using powders that stick to the oils left by fingers. Hairs, fibers, cigarettes, blood, weapons, and bullets are also part of the search. A detailed examination of the body and clothing is made to determine the points of entry and exit of the bullet. They look for gunpowder burns to indicate whether the gun was shot from a short distance. After they have looked at the evidence and sent samples to be analyzed by the forensic laboratory, they make a report to the homicide detective.

All of these procedures help to recreate the crime. The evidence can be used in court either to free or convict the defendant. If necessary, Detective Roussine may testify in court.

The tools pictured here are used by the forensic team to find fingerprints.

Trial   Felony defendants have the right to a trial by jury. In many cases they refuse that right, deciding instead to be tried by the judge. A criminal trial has several important characteristics. These are:

1. The defendant is assumed innocent until proven guilty.
2. To be found guilty there must be proof beyond a reasonable doubt.
3. The accused has a right not to take the stand and it will not be held against him or her.
4. Evidence obtained by the state in an illegal manner may not be used. (In some states, illegal evidence may be used but the person who obtains the evidence is punished.)
5. Use of the defendant's statements is allowed.

Sentencing   Normally, the judge has a great deal of freedom in deciding the sentence when a person has been found guilty. For most crimes, the judge has the choice of imposing imprisonment or probation. In many states, the legislature has set a maximum sentence for a certain crime. In some cases, the state laws have been declared unconstitutional by the United States Supreme Court. In those cases, the judge must go along with the ruling of the Supreme Court. The judge must confine his decision to these limitations.

Appeals Many defendants found guilty after their trial appeal their convictions. When they appeal, they are tried in an appellate court. This court reviews the results reached in prior trials in lower courts. The appellate court may change the decision of the lower court, or agree with it. The appellate court may also send the case back to the lower court for a new trial.

Post-conviction Remedies Adult felony prisoners often exercise their right to file **petitions,** or written requests, for **collateral relief.** This means that they can ask the federal court to decide whether steps taken in state courts are valid. The number of petitions from both state and federal prisoners has been steadily rising in the last several years. They are rarely successful.

SECTION checkup

1. What does arrest mean?
2. Who decides if a person should be arrested?
3. What is the purpose of having a grand jury in the criminal process?
4. List the different types of pleas a person being tried for a crime may enter.

4. YOUTH AND THE LAW

According to the Federal Bureau of Investigation, people under 18 years of age commit about one half of all serious crime in the United States. Fifteen-year-olds commit more serious crimes than any other age group. So it seems that the best starting point to attack crime is early in life.

Perhaps the most discouraging aspect of **juvenile delinquency** is the fact that a young person who gets into trouble with the law once is likely to do so again. In fact, studies have shown that juveniles are more likely to be returned to correctional institutions upon their release than are older offenders.

Responsibility for Crime A child who is too young to know the results of an act is not responsible for it. The child would not be criminally responsible if he or she was unable to tell right from wrong. Under the common law, a child under the age of seven is **conclusively presumed** to be incapable of committing a crime.

CASE STUDY

Susan is a fifteen-year-old girl living in an urban area. She has two brothers, aged 9 and 10, and a sister, aged 2. Her father is unemployed, and her mother cleans rooms in a local hospital. Susan's mother is very religious and has worked hard to provide for her family as best she can. The father is an alcoholic who appears to love his family when sober. He tends to lose control of himself when he has been drinking, which is often. He is angry with society and shows much of this anger against his wife. The two have frequent arguments and he often beats her.

The children are often witnesses to these fights. They were often beaten very harshly by their father for little things they did while he was drunk. The family lived in fear of the father. They never knew what to expect next.

On the particular night in question, the father came home drunk. The mother attempted to get him to go to bed and "sleep it off." The father refused. He grew tired of the insistence of his wife and he flew into a rage. He picked up a cast-iron skillet lying on the kitchen table. He threw it at her but missed. Susan was watching the incident. She realized that her father was out of control and she tried to stop him by jumping on his back. He threw her off and ran toward his wife. He knocked her down with his fist and picked up a chair and began hitting her with it. At this point Susan picked up the skillet and ran toward her father and struck him with all her might on his head. The father fell to the floor. Susan ran to the phone and called the police. Her father died on the way to the hospital. The mother was treated for bruises and released.

What will happen to Susan?

Children between seven and fourteen are thought to be incapable of committing a criminal act. If the government can prove that the child knew the nature and result of the act and could tell right from wrong, the child could be found guilty and punished.

Children over fourteen are thought to be able to commit a crime, but it is not conclusive. Therefore, the accused can make a case showing lack of ability to commit the crime and may win.

The **juvenile court** has jurisdiction over minors. The juvenile judge seeks to protect, educate, and rehabilitate the offender rather than punish. Steps followed by the court are less formal than those of a regular trial. There is no jury and little, if any, publicity in the press. Generally, names of minors are not given to the press and the trial is

Are children between seven and fourteen incapable of committing criminal acts such as petty theft?

often closed to the public. The judge makes the decision about the carrying out of justice. He or she is expected to exercise wisdom, patience and mercy.

Juvenile Court Judges   Juvenile court judges may decide the following in a case. They may deem a minor **a ward of the court, reprimand,** commit to a home or camp, assign a probation officer for guidance, or place in a certain type of **penal institution.**

Juveniles tend to be treated less harshly than adults for the same crime. Keep in mind that the juvenile court judge has the right to declare a person under 18 an adult. Then that individual can be tried as an adult. This may result from the number of times the juvenile has come before the court, or from the seriousness of the crime.

The Attitude of the Public   Generally speaking, the public has two attitudes toward the handling of youthful lawbreakers. There is a strong demand that authorities "get tough" with young hoodlums spoiled by the "softness" of the juvenile corrections system. There is also public anger over reports of harsh conditions in training schools (once called reform schools).

When someone is made a **ward of the court,** it means that the court acts in the place of the person's parents or guardian.

A **reprimand** (REH-pruh-mand) is a sharp rebuke.

Juveniles or minors must be given due process. In juvenile cases that may lead to commitment to an institution, the following requirements must be met:

1. Adequate notice must be given to the child and his or her parents long enough before the hearing to permit them to prepare for the case.
2. The child and the parents must be told of their right to be represented by counsel. If they cannot afford a lawyer, the court must appoint one.
3. The minor does not have to incriminate himself or herself.
4. The right to see witnesses against the minor and to have sworn testimony of those witnesses available for cross-examination.

Depending on the number of times a juvenile has been brought to court, a judge may decide to try him as an adult.

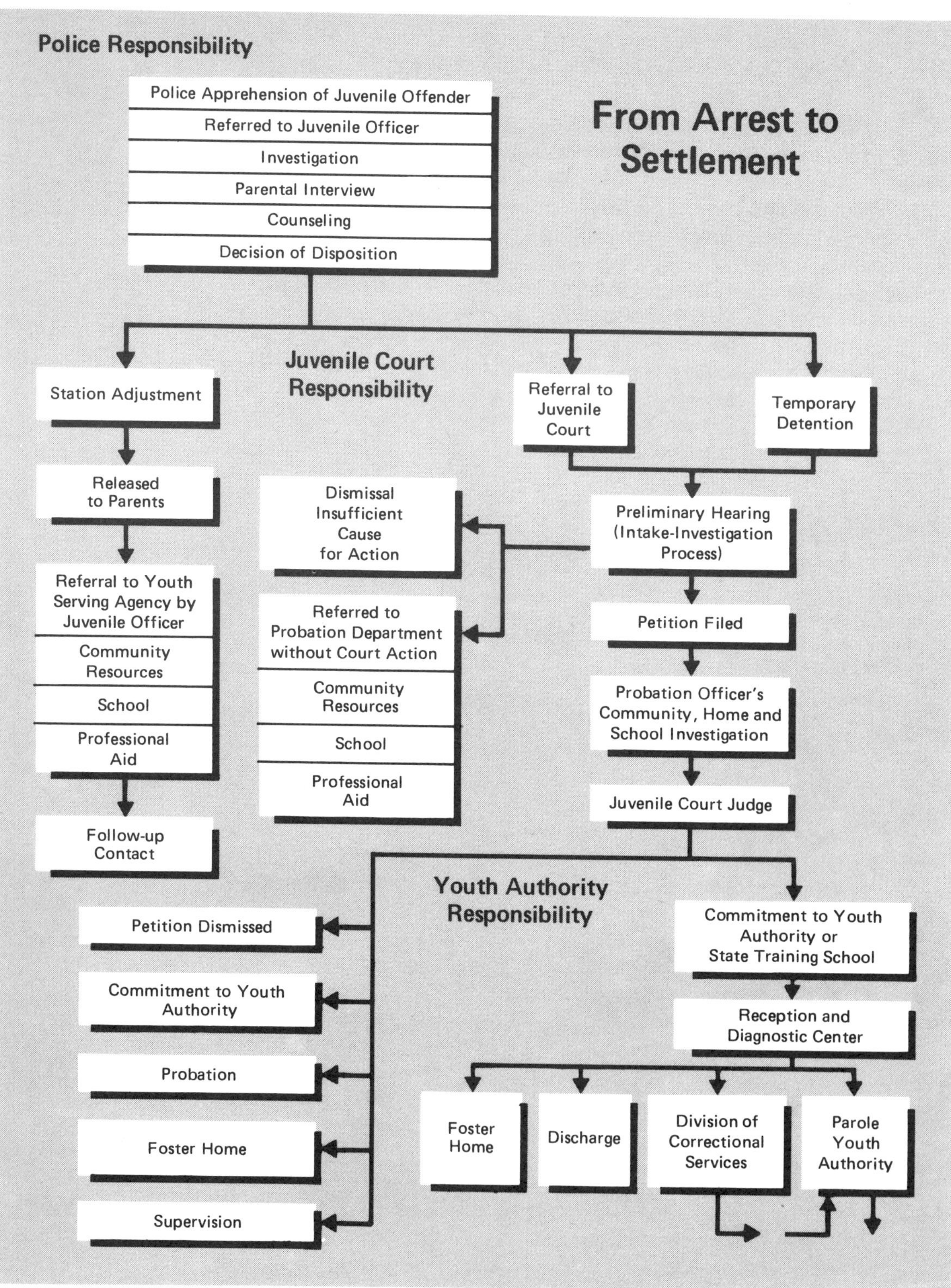
Police Responsibility
Police Apprehension of Juvenile Offender
Referred to Juvenile Officer
Investigation
Parental Interview
Counseling
Decision of Disposition
From Arrest to Settlement
Station Adjustment
Juvenile Court Responsibility
Referral to Juvenile Court
Temporary Detention
Released to Parents
Dismissal Insufficient Cause for Action
Preliminary Hearing (Intake-Investigation Process)
Referral to Youth Serving Agency by Juvenile Officer
Community Resources
School
Professional Aid
Referred to Probation Department without Court Action
Community Resources
School
Professional Aid
Petition Filed
Probation Officer's Community, Home and School Investigation
Follow-up Contact
Juvenile Court Judge
Youth Authority Responsibility
Petition Dismissed
Commitment to Youth Authority or State Training School
Commitment to Youth Authority
Reception and Diagnostic Center
Probation
Foster Home
Foster Home
Discharge
Division of Correctional Services
Parole Youth Authority
Supervision

In many states, juvenile records are confidential. The files are open only to police, probation officers, school officials, and employers. In most states a juvenile has the right to ask that personal records are sealed so that no one can examine them without a court order. However, the judge does not have to grant the petition. The decision of the judge is based on the individual petitioner. There may be a waiting period as long as five years after the last contact with the juvenile court before a juvenile can file the petition. Once juvenile records are officially sealed the juvenile no longer has a record. At this point a juvenile can legally answer "no" to the question "Have you ever been arrested?" Some applications for a professional license ask whether or not records have been sealed, and, if so, what circumstances surround the crime.

If Arrested, What Should You Do:
1. Be cooperative! Do not resist arrest or strike the officer.
2. Permit the officer to search you and your car.
3. Do not respond to questions until you are advised by an attorney. Answer only basic questions such as your name, address, and telephone number.
4. Permit fingerprinting when booked.
5. Request your right to make a telephone call. You should contact a person who can get a lawyer for you. This may be your parents, a relative, or a friend. If you are too poor to hire an attorney, ask the judge to get one for you.
6. If you have any physical handicap or a physical condition requiring medication, make this known.
7. Request your attorney to take steps to get your release.
8. It is important that you be honest with your attorney. Your conversations with the attorney are confidential.

SECTION CHECKuP

1. What does a juvenile judge do to help young people?
2. Do juveniles have the right to due process of law?
3. How is a juvenile's trial different from a trial for an adult?
4. What is probably the most discouraging aspect of juvenile crime?

CHAPTER REVIEW

Citizens of the United States are fortunate to have their basic freedoms guaranteed by the Constitution. One of the most important freedoms is that of safeguards against undue prosecution. Persons accused of crimes are assumed to be innocent until proven guilty. In many countries persons lose all their civil and political rights. They bear the burden of proving themselves innocent.

Each state has specific laws that say how persons accused of crimes are to be treated. This insures that the rights guaranteed by the Constitution of the United States are not violated. These processes are not exactly the same in every state, but they are very similar.

The Supreme Court of the United States has played a very important role in protecting our basic freedoms. An area that has received great attention lately has been due process of law for persons accused of a crime.

The most common types of crimes committed in this country are those against person, property, public health, safety and welfare, and public decency and morals. There is a wide variety of crimes in each of these categories. Adults are not the only persons guilty of these crimes. Juveniles commit large numbers of crimes every year. They must be dealt with in the juvenile court system. Due to their lack of maturity, minors are generally treated less harshly than adults. An effort is made to help them to become worthy citizens.

QUESTIONS FOR REVIEW

1. What is the basic philosophy of the Constitution about persons accused of a crime?
2. List each of the steps of the criminal process. Give a brief description of each step.
3. In what two amendments to the Constitution is the term "due process" used? What is the significance of its use the second time?
4. Trace each of the major events that led to the current use of the term "due process of law."
5. Describe how some states are affected by illegal smuggling of cigarettes.

1. **The Prosecutor.**   If a person was prosecuted for the crimes given below, would the crimes be listed as infractions, felonies, or misdemeanors? On a separate piece of paper, place an **I** for infraction, an **F** for felony, or an **M** for misdemeanor.

______ murder	______ disorderly conduct
______ shoplifting	______ manslaughter
______ assault	______ vagrancy
______ battery	______ robbery
______ breaking and entering	______ resisting arrest
______ car theft	______ destroying another's property
______ speeding	______ stealing
______ illegal parking	______ forgery
______ drunkenness	______ swindling
______ falsifying records	______ kidnapping
______ trespassing	______ hitchhiking on an interstate highway
______ littering on a public highway	______ cursing in public

2. Write a short paper defending your solution to the problem of crime and unpaid cigarette taxes.
3. Read the story of Susan in the section "Youth and the Law" very carefully. Trace each of the steps of the criminal process in which Susan would probably be involved.
4. Write a short paragraph describing what you think would be the outcome of Susan's case.

YOUR LAW LIBRARY

Clark, Todd (ed.), *Bill of Rights Newsletter.* Los Angeles, California: Constitutional Rights Foundation, Fall 1974.

Creamer, J. Shane, *A Citizen's Guide to Legal Rights.* New York: Holt, Rinehart and Winston, 1971.

Diamond, Robert A. and Arlene Alligood (eds.), *Crime and The Law.* Washington, D.C.: Congressional Quarterly, 1971.

MacNamara, Donald E. J. (ed.), *Readings in Criminal Justice 77/78.* Guilford, Connecticut: Duskin Publishing Group, Inc., 1977.

CORRECTIONS

chapter
5

Each of us has many choices every day. We choose whether or not to break the law. Each time you go into a store you decide to steal or not to steal something. Every time a person drives down the street, he or she chooses to break the law or not to break the law. A person may choose to run through a red light, or to stop. If you choose to break the law and are caught you will be punished by society. Society does this in order to protect citizens from the harm that lawbreakers cause.

There are many types of correctional methods for those who decide to break society's laws. **Probation** *is one of the less severe penalties; the lawbreaker serves little or no time in jail. Then there are different kinds of prisons where the criminal is sent according to the kind of crime committed. For some prisoners, there is the hope of rehabilitation. But for many others the dismal future that lies ahead is one of life in a small cell with none of the privacy or privileges enjoyed by the outside world. In this chapter you will learn about the steps involved in sentencing a criminal and how it is decided which means of correction that criminal will face.*

OBJECTIVES

To be able to list the purposes of the United States correctional system.

To describe the organization of correction systems.

To list the *pros* and *cons* of parole and probation.

To know the meaning of the term "capital punishment."

To list steps in the criminal process leading to a death sentence.

To describe arguments by those who are against capital punishment.

To know how the Supreme Court has ruled on capital punishment.

1. SENTENCING
2. CORRECTIONS SYSTEMS
3. PROBATION AND PAROLE
4. CAPITAL PUNISHMENT

---

1. SENTENCING

In the United States a person accused of a crime is brought to trial. There can only be two results of the trial; the accused person will be proven guilty or innocent. If an accused person's guilt has been proven during a trial, sentencing is the next step in the criminal process. Sentencing is also the first step in the **corrections process.** Corrections is a term used by the courts. It refers to all the procedures, facilities, and professionals who manage the problem of seeing that a criminal's sentence is served.

Deciding what Type of Sentence is Deserved   **Sentences** are clear definitions of the type of loss of freedom that a criminal will suffer as a result of having been found guilty. Who defines what type of loss of freedom a criminal will receive and for how long this loss of freedom will last?

People think of judges as handing down sentences from the "bench." Judges do pass sentence, but they have guidelines and help. Sentencing guidelines are built into almost all laws. A law may say the penalty for armed robbery in a state is not more than ten years and not less than three years of imprisonment. Judges in that state's courts have a sentencing guideline to follow. They must sentence persons convicted of armed robbery to terms of imprisonment between three and ten years.

Pre-sentence Reports   Before deciding upon an exact term for a particular person guilty of armed robbery, the judge will study a report called a **pre-sentence report.** This report has been written by the staff of the court. It is requested by the judge. It is an attempt to present to the judge a picture of the life-style of the convicted person. If the life-style pictured is that of a hardened criminal who has led others to commit crimes or who has a tendency to commit crimes of violence, the judge may decide to be severe and hand down the maximum sentence of ten years. If the life-style pictured to the judge is that of a person

An **accomplice** (uh-KOM-pliss) is one who helps plan or commit a crime or both.

who has usually been law-abiding and was led into this particular armed robbery by an **accomplice** who has a long criminal record, the judge may decide to be lenient. A lenient sentence would be the minimum of three years required by the statute.

Jury Sentencing In many states the judge is assisted by the jury in passing sentence. The jury that brings in a guilty verdict may suggest a sentence. The judge may then follow the jury's suggestion, or impose a sentence that is more lenient or more severe. Judges and juries may also share the sentencing duties. In cases where a person pleads guilty to a crime and no jury trial takes place, the judge passes sentence. In some states, if an accused person pleads innocent and goes to trial, the jury determines guilt or innocence as well as the sentence. The sentence must be within the limits set by the law the accused has been found guilty of violating. Some accused persons fear the severe sentences often imposed by juries. They decide to plead guilty in order to be sentenced by a judge who may be more lenient.

Purposes of a Sentence The public usually thinks of a sentence only as punishment. The corrections system is more than just the jails

A jury is supposed to represent the people in the community where a trial is being held. What groups are represented by this jury?

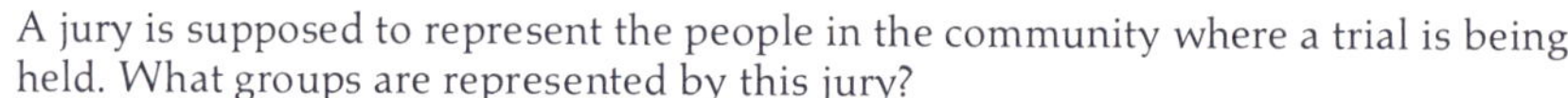

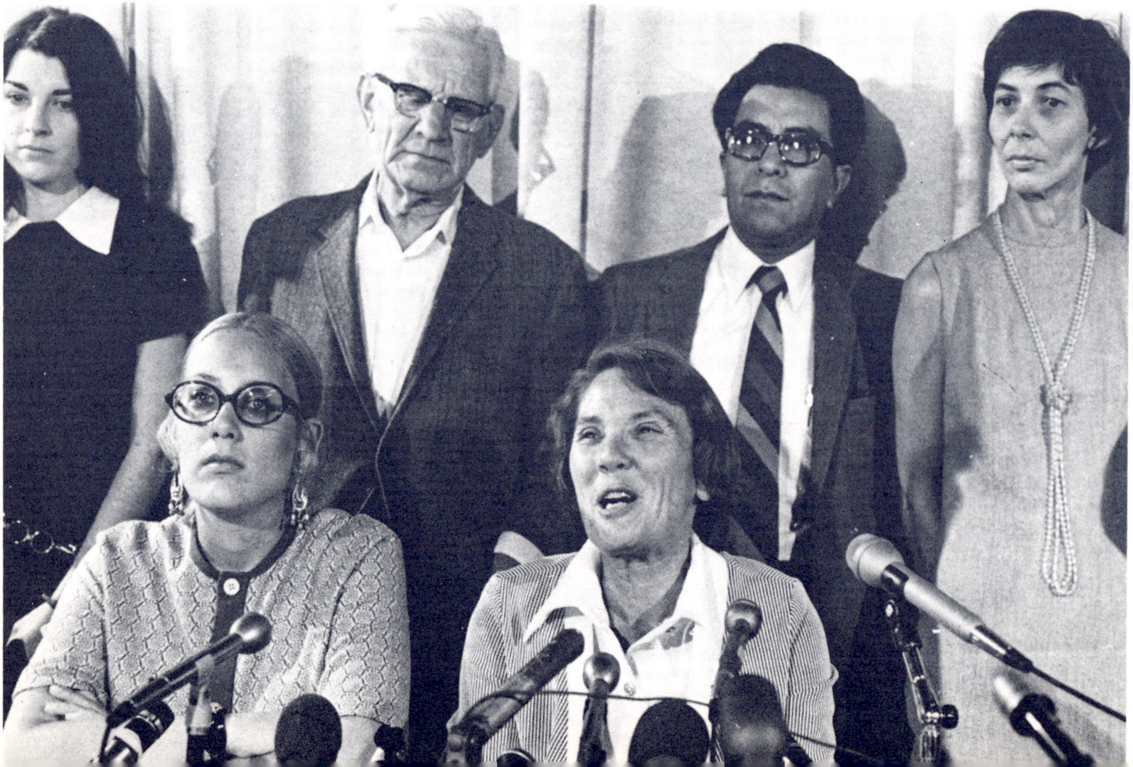

and prisons. Judges and correction staff are faced with the need to answer an important question: "What is the purpose of a sentence?"

There are three possible answers to this question. A sentence can be thought of as **retribution.** This is punishment that is society's revenge on the criminal for the harm that has been done. A sentence can be thought of as **deterrence.** This is punishment that is intended to prevent a criminal from committing a similar crime and to prevent other persons from committing similar crimes. A sentence can be thought of as **rehabilitation.** This is not as punishment at all but as a series of experiences that will help the convicted person avoid committing another crime of any type.

Deterrence   Most people in the United States today think that the threat of punishment acts as a **deterrent.** Parents keep young children from misbehaving by threatening punishment. When a child is naughty anyway, parents then punish the child. Suppose a father says to his son "Jack, I am going to spank you if you don't stop hitting your sister Jill." If Jack hits Jill again, he gets a spanking. The spanking is intended to help Jack decide not to hit Jill again. It is also to help Jack pay attention the next time his father threatens punishment for breaking rules. Suppose there is a third child in their family. If you were the brother or sister of Jack and Jill, how would Jack's spanking make you feel? Would you be less likely to hit Jill after having seen Jack get a spanking for hitting her? Would you be more likely to follow your family's rules after seeing your brother punished for disobeying one of them? This is a way of viewing a sentence or a punishment as deterrence.

There are some problems with using punishment as a deterrent. First, if you are a brother or sister to Jack and Jill, you have to believe you will be caught or else you won't be deterred by the threat of a spanking. Second, you have to be afraid of the spanking. If you aren't bothered by spanking, you may be willing to suffer one just to have the fun of hitting Jill. Third, you may hit Jill in a fit of temper when you have forgotten all about getting a spanking.

Weaknesses of Deterrence   The court and correction staff who are in favor of viewing a sentence as rehabilitation rather than deterrence usually question whether or not sentences really act as deterrents. Research shows that people who plan crimes in advance never believe they are going to be caught. Actually most crimes in our society are never reported to the police. Unless the police can catch most of those who commit crimes, the threat of punishment will deter only those criminals who have been caught and punished at least once.

Research also shows that, while we are all reluctant to give up our freedom, most first offenders have no real idea of what going to jail or prison is like. How can a person be deterred by the threat of going to jail if that person knows nothing about life in jail? Also a great many crimes of violence are committed in a fit of anger or passion. At the moment these crimes are committed, the criminals are so angry or excited that they never think of the possibility of being sent to prison as a punishment for what they are doing.

Rehabilitation   As society has become more aware of reasons why punishment as a deterrent might not work, another purpose for imprisonment has been worked out. In the last 100 years, many corrections authorities have come to favor **rehabilitation** rather than punishment. Rehabilitation is helping make a better society by helping criminals learn to "go straight." It tries to keep them from committing other crimes once they are set free. It has been advocated as a positive approach to correction. The corrections staff who favor rehabilitation hope that criminals will "go straight" because they want what society gives to law-abiding citizens.

What changes must be made in criminals to rehabilitate them? Corrections officials who have tried to design and run prisons where criminals would be rehabilitated have tried different answers to this question. Many criminals were found to be uneducated. Some were even unable to read and write. So, prison schools have become a part of rehabilitation programs. Many criminals were also found to have been unable to get or hold a job. As a result, vocational training has become a central part of rehabilitation programs. Many criminals were found to have been in poor mental health. So, psychological counseling to help prisoners get over their "hang-ups" has become a part of rehabilitation programs. Certain features of old-style prisons handicapped prisoners upon their release into society. As a result, building and managing prisons so that life within them will be less regimented and less likely to cause prisoners to resent authority has become a part of the rehabilitation effort.

Weakness of Rehabilitation   Rehabilitation is an attempt to change negative values prisoners have toward society. Many prisons and prison programs are devoted to this goal. Rehabilitation has not been widely accepted by the public. Crime is much more frequent in our society now than it was when the idea of rehabilitation was first introduced. Rehabilitation programs are not responsible for the increase in crime in modern America. Many legislators are beginning to think that the failure of rehabilitation has weakened the deterrent effect of sentences of imprisonment. Many people now support the older idea of imprisonment purely for its deterrent effect on criminals.

Deterrence vs. Rehabilitation   Today, there is an argument in the corrections system. Some people believe in punishment for deterrence. Others believe in punishment for rehabilitation. This struggle is seen in disagreements on two important issues. One issue asks the question

Vocational training is often needed in order for prisoners to get jobs once they are released.

"What type of sentences should be given?" The other issue asks the question "What type of prisons and prison programs should be constructed and maintained?"

Those in favor of sentences as deterrents usually favor "flat time" or at least mandatory minimum sentences. This means that every person convicted of the same crime would have to serve the same minimum sentence. The convicted person's life-style would not affect the sentence. The prisons in which "flat time" sentences would be served would have deterrence as their main purpose. Prisoners would attend only those rehabilitation programs for which they volunteered. No

 ON CAREERS

Counselors and Psychologists

Mental health problems are frequent among prisoners. Many prisoners have committed crimes partly because of serious mental health problems. Jail causes other prisoners to develop extreme mental stress.

Counselors and psychologists work with prisoners in classification centers in order to determine what types of rehabilitation programs are best for each inmate. Counselors and psychologists work in regular prisons to help prisoners adjust to prison life. Helping prisoners prepare themselves to resume a normal life outside prison is also an important duty of psychologists and counselors.

To become a counselor or psychologist you must finish college. To be a registered psychologist you must go on from college to graduate school, for two or three more years. Since many prisons need additional trained counselors and psychologists, there are many good job opportunities for people to work in prisons.

Dr. Melvin Kaye is Chief Psychologist for the New York City Department of Prison Health Services. One of his most important jobs has been to help prisoners during their pretrial periods. During pretrial periods, prisoners are usually very nervous because they are unsure about what will happen to them. Two other problems that Dr. Kaye helps prisoners with are (1) learning to live in prison where there is no freedom, and (2) helping prisoners return to lives outside once they are released. Dr. Kaye says that many prisoners are afraid to go back to lives outside of prisons because they become used to having everything done for them. Therefore, they misbehave when released in order to return to prison.

Dr. Kaye sees his job as a challenging one but he also admits that the job is not easy.

schooling, psychological counseling, or vocational training would be required. Prisoners would have to rehabilitate themselves. They would serve a longer "flat time" sentence for a repeat conviction of the same or similar crime.

Advocates of rehabilitation are in favor of sentences as **indeterminate,** or unspecified, periods of time. The sentence would be served in a setting (not necessarily a prison) that would make rehabilitation

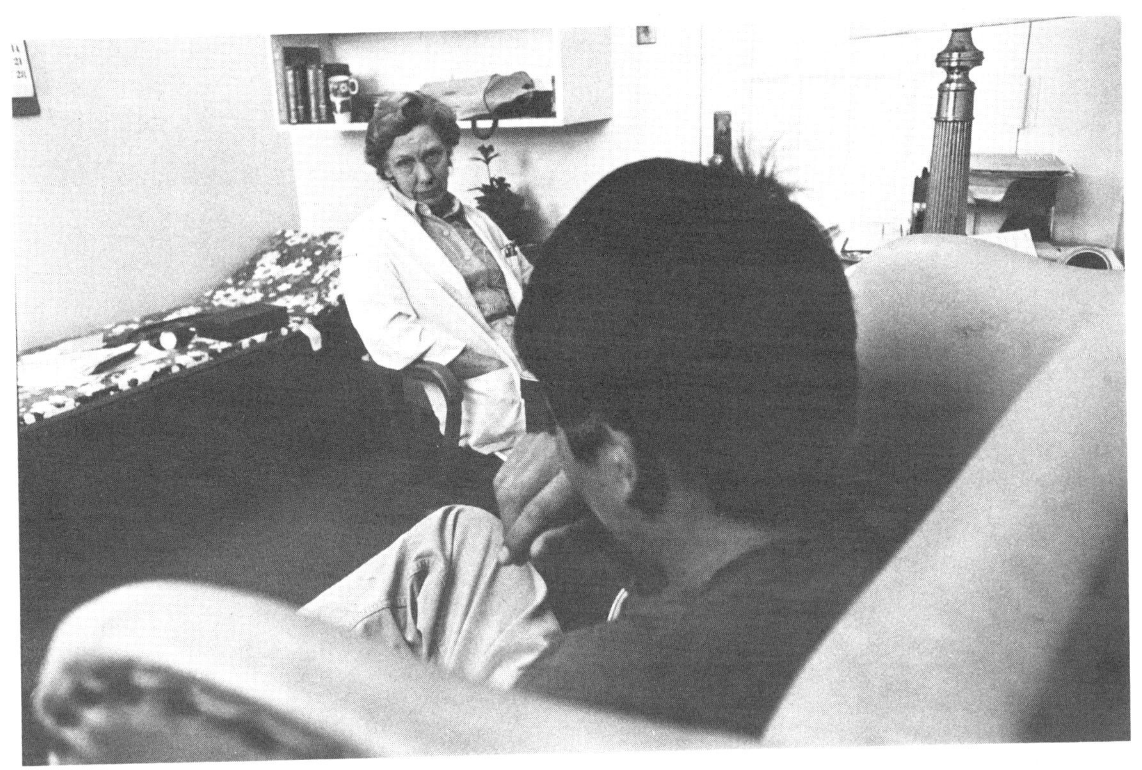

Counselors and psychologists help prisoners adjust to prison life.

likely. When an inmate has shown readiness for a normal life as a productive person, his or her case would be brought before a group known as a parole board. The parole board would review all the facts of the case, as well as the inmate's behavior in prison, and decide if the inmate is really ready to be released.

SECTION CHECKUP

1. What is the purpose of a **pre-sentence report?**
2. What three possible purposes may a sentence serve?
3. How are **retribution** and **deterrence** different?
4. What is **rehabilitation?**
5. How is **rehabilitation** different from deterrence?
6. What circumstances can prevent a threat of punishment from having a deterrent effect?

2. CORRECTIONS SYSTEMS

In the United States, persons caught by the police for breaking a local law will be tried in a local court. If they break a state law, they are tried in a state court. If they break a federal law, they are tried in a federal court. Each of the three jurisdictions—local, state, or federal—must maintain some type of corrections system. Because the three types of jurisdictions are connected in certain ways, the corrections systems maintained by each jurisdiction are also connected. Most local courts act as the first level in the state court system. Even though a person has been accused of violating a state law, the trial may take place in a local court. The sentence imposed by a judge may be served in either a local correctional facility or in a state correctional facility.

Jails   Local correctional facilities are usually called **jails.** Jails are designed to house prisoners serving sentences of one year or less. They house prisoners who are awaiting their first hearing after arrest. They also house those who have been denied bail while waiting for their trial. Most places have only one jail. Large cities may have several because there are more crimes committed and more trials held. In the past, punishment was thought of as the jail's purpose. Today most jails have programs to rehabilitate their prisoners. Such programs include classes in everything from reading to psychology. Many jails also have education release and work release programs. For example, an inmate who has a job outside the jail Monday through Friday but who remains in jail at night and on weekends is said to be on work release. An inmate who goes to school outside the jail is on education release.

All jails are required to have separate facilities for men and women as well as for adults and juveniles. Most jails also separate felons from those who have committed misdemeanors.

Jails are paid for and run by local governments; they are carefully regulated by state governments. This is done to make sure that all jails in a state meet minimum standards of health and safety. Jails are required to provide prisoners with nutritious meals, proper clothing, sanitary facilities and other necessities.

State Corrections Systems   State corrections systems are larger and more varied than local systems. There are usually prisons for women with separate facilities for juveniles. A **maximum security prison** houses criminals who are serving long terms for violent felonies. These prisons often have a section called "death row"—for pris-

There is little privacy in jail. This picture shows how small and dreadful a jail cell can be.

oners awaiting execution. A **medium security prison** houses criminals who have committed less severe crimes but who are serving long sentences. Their prospects for rehabilitation are poor.

Maximum and medium security prisons usually look like fortresses. They are surrounded by high walls with watchtowers with armed sentries. Armed guards also patrol the grounds, the cellblocks where prisoners live, exercise areas, dining halls, and the prison hospital. Prisoners in such facilities usually spend long hours—perhaps 16 hours a day—in their cells. Exercise and recreation are limited. Privacy is almost non-existent. Rehabilitation facilities in these prisons concentrate on reading and basic skills.

State correctional systems also have **minimum security facilities,** work camps, prison farms, and work release centers. A modern minimum security prison may look like a campus surrounded by a high, wire fence. These facilities house first and second offenders who can benefit from rehabilitation programs.

Paramedic

Whether they live in normal society or are confined in prison, people have health problems. In a jail too small to have a full-time doctor, prisoners with major injuries or illnesses are taken away from jail to a local hospital for medical care. Prisoners with minor injuries or illnesses can be treated by a nurse or a paramedic in the jail dispensary. Prisoners placed on medication after a doctor's examination come to the dispensary to get medication.

Paramedics are usually supervised by a registered nurse. They are also known as physician assistants. To become a paramedic you must graduate from high school. You must then attend a junior or community college that has a program designed to train paramedics. Most programs last at least two years. After graduation a paramedic can work in a fire department, hospital, clinic, or prison.

Although there are jobs in cities, the physician assistant program is basically designed for people to work in rural areas where there are not many physicians available.

Dave O'Hanlon is a paramedic at Rikers Island Prison infirmary. He began his studies at the Public Health Service Hospital in Staten Island, New York. After completing two years of courses in anatomy, microbiology, physiology, and other medically-related courses, he received his state certificate.

Mr. O'Hanlon begins his day at work by examining new patients and writing down their medical histories. Then he orders tests to help him make a diagnosis. In addition, he follows up on other patients by examining them and reviewing their progress. When the test results that he orders on new patients are ready, he studies them and decides what medication and treatment should be given. All of his duties are monitored and supervised by the physician on duty.

Minimum security prisons usually have extensive vocational training programs. These may include shops where prisoners learn a trade. For example, if a minimum security prison houses 3,000 prisoners it must serve 9,000 meals each day. The job of preparing these meals will be managed by a few vocational teachers who use it as an opportunity to teach inmates the skills for feeding thousands of people.

Prisoners learn to be meat cutters, bakers, short-order cooks, restaurant managers, or many of the other skilled trades involved in large-scale food preparation. Minimum security prisoners also have shops where prisoners learn such skilled trades as carpentry, cabinet-making, metal working, or auto mechanics. Often, graduation from one of the vocational skills programs is required before a prisoner may be paroled from such a facility.

Minimum security prisons also have recreation facilities such as gyms and playing fields. Teams of prisoners compete with teams from other prisons and also with local community teams. Drama groups and painting studios are common in minimum security prisons. Drug abuse counseling programs are available. Sometimes inmates who are rehabilitated drug addicts form counseling teams. They travel outside the facility to present programs about the dangers of drug abuse to high schools, civic clubs, and organizations.

Prisoners are often responsible for preparing the meals of their fellow inmates.

Work release facilities are features of state corrections systems. A work release facility often looks like a motel. There are separate rooms for prisoners, game rooms, a cafeteria, and a kitchen. There are also offices for vocational and job counselors who help the inmates. The prisoners are still serving their terms, but they are released into the community to work on regular jobs. Inmates of work release facilities have been judged ready to make the transition from prison back into a normal, productive life in their communities.

Many prisoners are transferred to a work release facility from some other facility within the state. A male prisoner serving a ten-year term for a second offense of armed robbery is sent to a medium security prison. After spending three years in the prison school, he is moved to a minimum security prison. There he goes to work in the food preparation area. He learns to be a baker or a chef. Then a job counselor may locate a job for him with a local bakery or restaurant. If the prisoner can be paroled within 12 to 18 months, he may go to a work release facility where he will live and be supervised in his job until his parole. In a case such as this, a state corrections system is trying to do two things: to punish the prisoner for his offense against society and to prepare him to return to society with the skills and values he needs to avoid committing additional crimes.

Classification Centers   A successful state corrections system depends on many things. Each person in prison must be placed in that part of the state's corrections system best suited to his or her needs and abilities. Judges do not decide where a prisoner will be sent. Before states developed different types of prisons, this problem did not exist. Today it is necessary for a good state system to have a **classification center.**

After sentence is imposed a prisoner is sent to the classification center. At the classification center counselors and psychologists, examine the prisoner's background and potential. Tests are given to determine what sort of personality the prisoner has developed. Achievement tests are used to measure the prisoner's educational level, vocational abilities, and desires. With this information and the pre-sentence report, the staff of the classification center can decide where the prisoner will begin to serve his or her sentence.

Federal Corrections Facilities   The federal corrections system is comprehensive. It has classification centers, work release centers, minimum, medium, and maximum security facilities. The whole system is run by the United States Bureau of Prisons headquartered in Washington, D.C. Persons convicted and sentenced in federal courts serve their sentences in facilities run by the Bureau of Prisons. These facilities are scattered around the whole country. Often, the minimum security facilities use buildings originally built for housing soldiers on military bases.

In addition to running a comprehensive system, the Bureau of Prisons is supposed to design and create facilities that can serve as models of the best corrections practices. New federal prisons often illustrate the latest methods of building design. They often try new methods of managing prison populations or rehabilitation techniques. Federal prisons often serve as centers for important research conducted by correction authorities or **criminologists.** A criminologist is one who researches various aspects of crime to discover why crimes take place and how to prevent them.

Recidivism   Whether we see the purpose as deterrence or rehabilitation, it would seem that one sentence would be enough to keep people from committing further crimes. However, this is not true. Over half of the people who are in prison in the United States today are serving a second, third, fourth, or even fifth term. In the language of corrections authorities these prisoners are **recidivists.**

Researchers have been trying to determine just what sort of prison environment turns people into recidivists, or "repeaters." Up to now no really successful solutions to the problem have been discovered. The rates of recidivism in all types of correctional facilities continue to be very high.

Recidivism is costly to society. The damage caused by the crime costs money because of new trials. It is also very expensive to keep a person in prison.

SECTION CHECKUP

1. Why can a person accused of violating a state law be tried in a local court?
2. Why are very secure prison facilities needed?
3. Name and briefly describe the appearance of three different types of prisons.
4. How do **minimum** and **maximum security prisons** differ?
5. Describe a work release facility.
6. What is the purpose of a **classification center?**
7. Write a brief paragraph illustrating the meaning of the term **recidivism.**
8. List four jobs that a prisoner can learn while in prison.

3. PROBATION AND PAROLE

Probation and parole are types of relief from the punishment of being confined in a prison cell. **Probation** is a type of sentence. If someone is put on probation he or she must be supervised for a certain period of time. Supervision is done by an officer of the court that sentenced the person. During the period of probation the person is expected to behave correctly and to check in with the officer at certain specified times. Violation of probation can result in the revocation, or cancellation, of probation. If this happens, the person is re-sentenced to a prison term.

Parole is the reduction of a prison sentence. The possibility of being paroled is a legal part of most sentences. When a person is sentenced to

This is a copy of a fake parole certificate. What does this certificate tell you about the person it was written for?

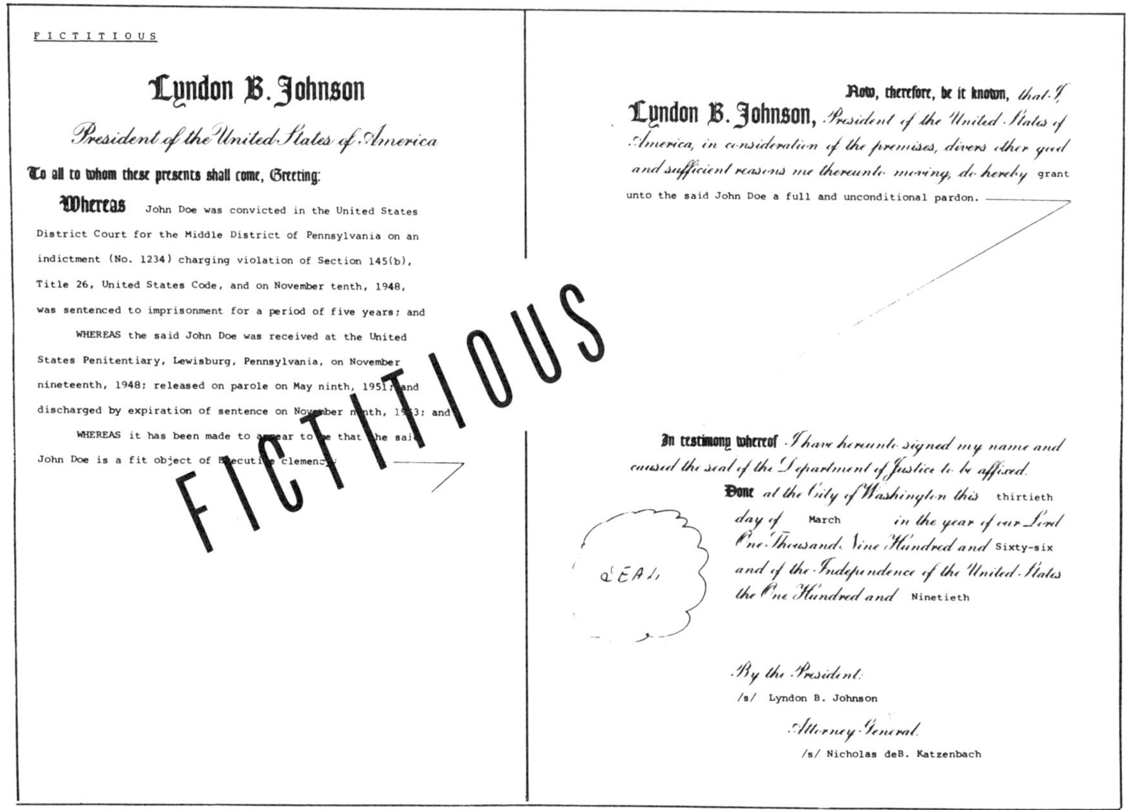

ONE STEP BEYOND—
"TODAY'S PRISON OF THE FUTURE"

Many experts on corrections believe that prisons will change dramatically within the next 10-15 years. One man, Norval Morris, is widely thought of as an expert. He plans future prisons. In his book, **The Future of Imprisonment,** he explains what differences he envisions. Morris believes, for example, that indeterminate sentences, paroles and parole boards, harsh treatment, loss of privacy, mandatory rehabilitation practices, and large prisons are on the way out. They will be replaced by small prison units, humane treatment of inmates, fixed sentences, voluntary rehabilitation programs and extensive programs of work and education release.

In 1977, the United States Bureau of Prisons had five new model prisons in various stages of construction. All of these units are modeled after the most experimental prison in the federal corrections system—the Federal Correctional Institute at Butner, North Carolina. Opened on May 13, 1976, Butner embodies some of Morris's views on prisons of the future. It was designed to hold 200 male inmates rather than the thousands that are held in the federal "big houses" at Marion, Leavenworth, and Atlanta. Butner has individual furnished rooms instead of cells, shared television lounges, and recreation rooms. Each prisoner occupies a room for which he has the key. Guards can check on a prisoner's presence by looking through a small window in the door of each room. The fence around the entire complex is patrolled by guards driving cars along a paved road. No bars, walls, or gun towers are needed. The front entrance has no guard. It has only a closed circuit television camera.

Butner has had problems. Few prisoners are pleased with the rehabilitation programs there. Work and study release programs are available on a limited basis. Staff members, half of whom are women, are unhappy with working conditions. Three different directors have headed the complex in less than two years. The Bureau of Prisons has thought of assigning 150 more inmates to Butner. This would change most of the single rooms into doubles. This destroys the idea of privacy which was so important to the original design of the facility. The degree to which Butner can overcome its problems may well serve as a guide to the direction prison reform will take in the United States in the coming years.

The federal prison in Butner, North Carolina is one of the new model correctional facilities.

25 years in prison, the law will state that the person becomes eligible for parole when 15 years of the sentence have been served. Becoming eligible for parole does not mean that a prisoner will be paroled. Awarding of parole is in the hands of a **parole board.** They rule "yes" or "no" on each case brought before it. It bases its decision on factors such as whether the prisoner seems capable of leading a crime-free life and the severity of the crime for which the person was imprisoned.

If the parole board decides "yes," the prisoner is then released on parole. This means that he or she promises the court—in writing—to follow a set of rules. In return, the court has the duty of supervising the **parolee** for a period of not more than five years. An officer of the court, called a **parole officer,** is in charge of watching the parolee. As with probation, the parolee must check in with the officer at certain times. Violation of parole can result in return to prison. This often happens in cases where the violator is convicted, or even accused of another crime.

The Purposes of Probation and Parole Both probation and parole are alternatives to imprisonment. Probation is common for first offenses of crimes that are not serious. If a young person is arrested for possessing marijuana, the judge will often sentence him or her to probation. This is done because the judge decides that imprisoning the person will result in no good, either to the person or to society. Prison might possibly result in harm. Parole is used to give prisoners a chance to adjust to the problems of life in society. Without parole, there would be no period of supervised transition from prison to ordinary life. Parole helps prisoners who are clearly rehabilitated win release after serving part of their sentences.

Problems with Probation   Both probation and parole are controversial issues. People who run the nation's corrections systems disagree as to whether either one really accomplishes its purpose.

There are at least two problems with probation. One is that probation officers often have to work with too many persons. A probation officer with a case load of 50 or more probationers cannot offer real help to those being supervised. In such a situation, probation is a formality. It fails to rehabilitate or to deter. Another problem arises when

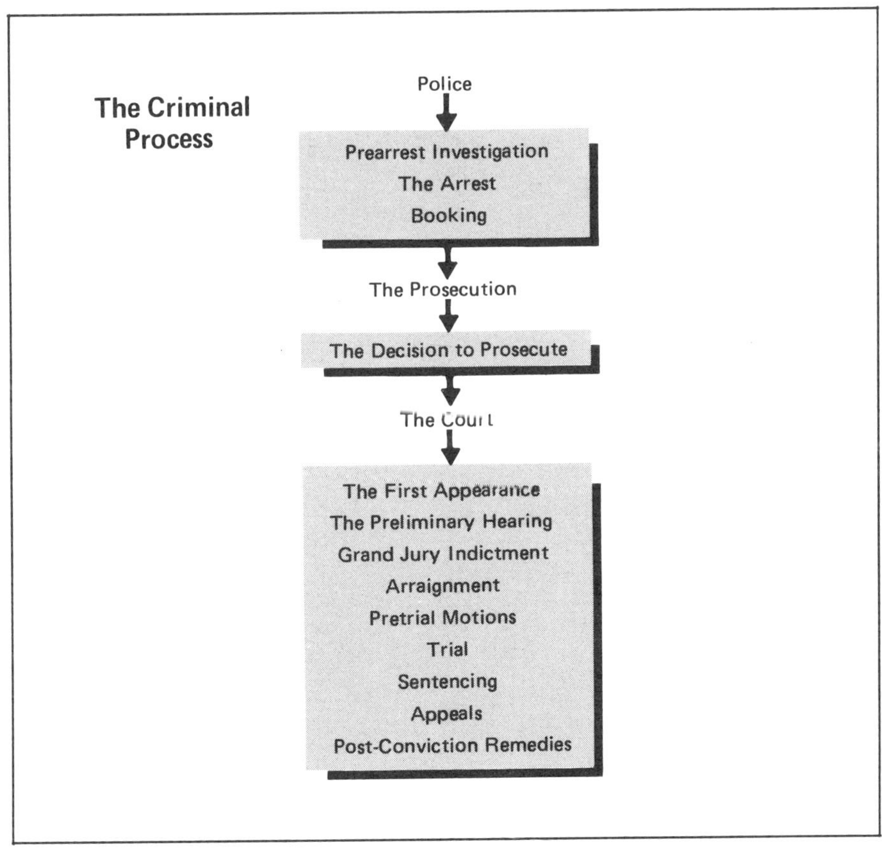

prisoners are crowded. More and more persons who have been convicted are placed on probation rather than in prison. In such a situation, courts lose part of their ability to deter crime since many criminals are not frightened by the threat of being on probation. When many criminals who have no desire to reform are placed on probation, the task of the probation officer becomes impossible.

Problems with Parole   Parole presents other problems. Fairness is one of these. Most prisoners expect the parole board to be fair in considering each case. Often they are disappointed. The board will refuse to grant parole for some reason which, in the prisoner's eyes, has nothing to do with his or her case. To be fair the board must try to treat similar cases in the same way. However, this is not as easy as it may

James LeBouef escaped from prison in Michigan. The courts dismissed his case because he had lived a good life since the time he escaped. LeBouef's secret life as an escapee was discovered when he tried to help a policeman whom he thought was in trouble.

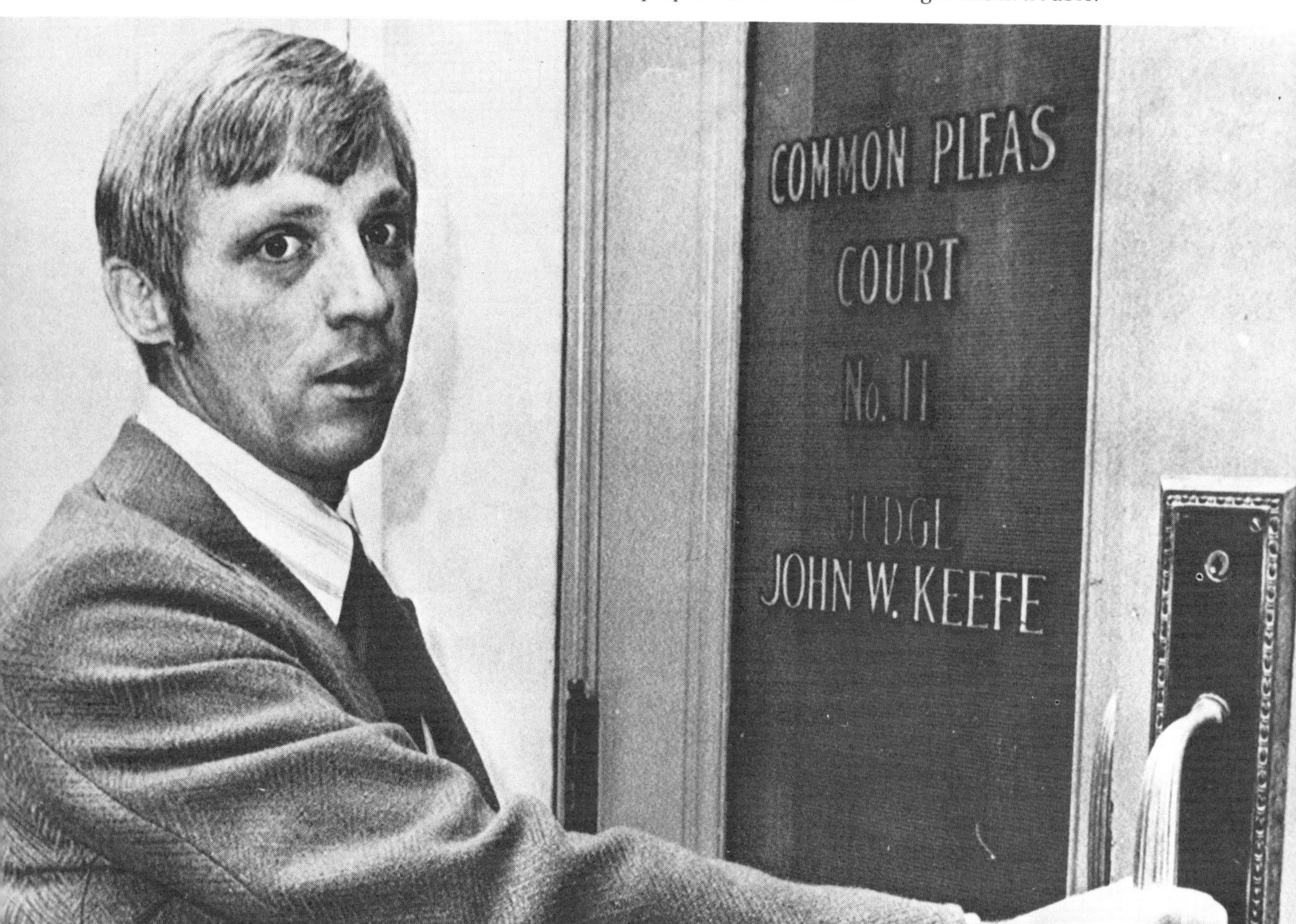

seem. For example, if two persons committed armed robbery (robbery with a weapon) they have theoretically committed the same crime. The parole board might grant parole to the person who committed an armed robbery in which no physical injury was caused and deny it to the person who committed armed robbery in which the weapon was used to harm others.

Parole boards also face the hard job of predicting who will adjust well to life in society and who will probably not. This is a difficult task because many corrections officials believe that a person's ability to adjust to prison life does not indicate how well he or she will adjust to life outside prison.

The attitude of the public toward parole is still another problem. Often, the public will feel that parole is unfair leniency. This is because the public usually hears about parole when something has gone wrong, not when it is going well. If a person is free on parole and commits a violent crime, it is news. The media informs the public. There are suggestions that the person should not have been freed in the first place. It is obvious to the public that the crime would not have been committed had the person been kept in prison.

Recently, there has been a strong demand for more severe treatment of persons convicted of crimes. This has resulted in longer sentences. Without the parole system each criminal would serve the whole sentence imposed by the judge. This would mean many more persons in prison. Then, many more prisons would have to be built at great cost to taxpayers.

Corrections people believe that no good purpose is served by years of confinement. After a certain length of time in prison, a person is either rehabilitated or will never be. Parole makes it possible to release those who have been rehabilitated and to separate them from prisoners who cannot be. Prisoners who cannot be rehabilitated may have a very destructive influence on those who do have real potential for rehabilitation.

SECTION CheckUp

1. Define **probation** and **parole**. What is the difference between them?
2. Why are probation and parole controversial?
3. What do you think would happen to the corrections system if probation and parole were stopped?
4. Why is it difficult for parole boards to be fair?
5. What are some duties of a parole officer?

Probation or Parole Officers

Many persons who are convicted of non-serious crimes are placed on probation by a judge. Many persons who are sentenced to a prison term are released on parole after serving a part of that term. If you are on probation or parole, you have agreed to a set of terms or conditions. These terms are designed to insure that you will be a productive, law-abiding citizen while free on probation or parole.

Probation and parole officers have two duties. One is to help offenders abide by the terms of their probation or parole agreement. This means helping men and women guilty of crimes learn how to lead a law-abiding life.

The other duty of probation and parole officers is to maintain contact between the court and the offender on probation or parole. From time to time, the officer certifies to the court that the conditions of probation or parole are being met. If an offender violates the set of conditions established by the court, the officer can suggest that probation or parole be revoked.

To become a probation or parole officer you must be able to help people adjust to living in a group. One way to acquire the necessary qualifications is to go to college and major in sociology or social work. You can also study psychology and counseling in order to become a probation or parole officer. To succeed as a probation or parole officer you must be good at relating to people.

Elayne Neufeld, a supervising probation officer, has worked with the New York City Department of Probation for ten years. As a probation officer, she helped investigate and interview defendants. She then recommended to the court whether the defendant should be placed on probation or go to jail. She worked with an average of 100 probationers from one to five years to help them adjust to their environment. Many of the probationers had a history of failure in life and a very low self-image. Ms. Neufeld found it necessary to help probationers acquire the skills to get a good job and to feel better about themselves. This was accomplished by counseling and referring them to various social service agencies.

Ms. Neufeld also watched over her probationers' progress. She visited them at their jobs and homes, checked their continued employment, and maintained an up-to-date file on their residence. She was notified if any probationers were involved in any trouble by the police.

A probation officer requires patience and understanding. Ms. Neufeld feels satisfied when her probationers make progress.

Rehabilitated prisoners set up this store called the Fortune Store. What ideas are conveyed by different items in this picture?

4. CAPITAL PUNISHMENT

Punishment for crime was a public event in colonial times. Petty thieves were put in the stocks on the public square or whipped in public. Murderers were hanged. Hangings were often public events attended by men, women, and children. It was generally accepted that hanging a criminal publicly kept others from committing the same type of crime. Today punishment for crime is private. Going to prison means being shut away from public view. Executions are seen by only a few persons such as prison wardens and chaplains. Although they could be, executions are not televised.

Methods of execution have changed too. Hangings where the victim took twenty minutes to strangle led many citizens to demand a more "humane" method of killing. So death in the electric chair and death in the gas chamber were introduced in many states. Because there have been few witnesses to such executions, the general public has been able to assume that these methods result in instant death and are less cruel than hanging. This is not always the case.

Changes in Capital Punishment   A dramatic decline in the number of executions in the United States per year has occurred since 1960. During the 1950s about seventy executions per year took place. In the 1960s, only about twenty executions took place each year. Between 1965 and 1969, only ten men and no women were executed in the United States. Since 1970 there have been a number of years in which no executions took place. In 1977 only one state, Utah, executed a man, Gary Gilmore.

Why have these changes taken place? In order to understand why capital punishment has nearly been abolished we must look at two of the amendments to the Constitution. The Eighth Amendment forbids "cruel and unusual" punishment and the Fourteenth Amendment forbids states or the federal government to deprive citizens of life, liberty, or property without due process of law. How these amendments are seen by the Supreme Court determines whether or not capital punishment will be permitted and, if permitted under what conditions it may take place.

Until the 1960s the Supreme Court had never seriously considered abolishing capital punishment on the Eighth Amendment grounds that it was "cruel and unusual." It was certainly unusual in the sense that executions did not often happen. Death was a cruel form of punishment in Western society.

Up until the 1960s, the Supreme Court only ruled on the appeals of death sentences brought by individual inmates awaiting execution.

Events Leading to a Death Sentence   When the Supreme Court rules on such an appeal the ruling is the final step in a process that begins when a state legislature passes a law allowing the death penalty for an offense. Murder with malice has most often been the crime in which a death sentence can be imposed.

The second step in the process is catching and charging the person with the crime. After a person has been charged with a capital crime the prosecutor must decide whether or not to ask the jury for the death penalty. **Extenuating circumstances**—for instance, if the person who has been murdered had previously threatened the accused murderer with bodily harm—may cause the prosecutor not to request the death penalty. The mental and physical condition of the defendant may also cause a prosecutor not to request the death penalty. In the case of **heinous** crimes, death penalties have often been requested.

Heinous crimes (HAY-nus)—A heinous crime is one that is particularly brutal, cruel, unpredictable, and shocking to the community in which it is committed.

CASE STUDY

Suppose a local hoodlum murdered a 15-year-old girl because her father testified against him in a trial for auto theft. If you were the prosecutor would you ask for the death penalty?

A trial in which the death penalty is sought is the third step in the process. In such a trial the physical evidence is often overwhelming. In many cases, the accused may have been apprehended at the scene of the crime with a "smoking gun" in hand. Or, the accused may have confessed while being questioned by the police. Often, the real question at issue in the trial is whether the accused will get life imprisonment or a death sentence.

In such cases, choosing the jury is an important part of the trial procedures. The prosecution can exclude some jurors that it believes will not vote for conviction. The defense can exclude jurors that it believes will not vote to acquit the accused. The purpose of this is to make sure that the jury is as fair as possible. For many years judges allowed prosecutors to exclude from such juries anyone who expressed even a general objection to capital punishment.

This door leads to the execution room in the Washington State Penitentiary.

At the end of a capital case, the judge instructs the jury in the meaning of the law and informs them that in the case of a guilty verdict they may recommend either death or life imprisonment. A jury can find a person guilty of a capital offense and sentence the accused to be executed. The process of appealing the sentence can begin at this point.

Appeal of a Death Sentence   In a narrow, specific sense the purpose of the appeals process is to see if any mistakes were made in the defendant's trial. In a general sense the appeals process is used to see if the defendant had a fair trial. If the court with jurisdiction over the appeal finds that enough errors were made so that the trial was not fair, the appeals court may require a new trial or it may choose to change the death sentence to life imprisonment.

Since most capital offenses are violations of state rather than federal laws, a person sentenced to death first appeals in state courts. If the highest appeal court in that state denies the appeal, two other possibilities exist. One is to request the governor of the state to grant **executive clemency.** This changes the prisoner's sentence to life imprisonment. Another is to take advantage of the Fourteenth Amendment's order that the states not deprive any citizens of life, liberty, or property without due process of law. Inmates sentenced to death can appeal their sentences in the federal court system on the ground that mistakes in their original trials were such that **"due process"** was not provided.

136

The federal courts are a three-level system. Any appeal of a death sentence begins in Federal District Court. If denied there, it goes next to a Federal Court of Appeals. If denied in the Court of Appeals, it may possibly go to the Supreme Court.

The Supreme Court does not hear every case that is appealed to it. Instead, the justices look at the cases and select those that deserve a final hearing. In the 1960s the justices selected a few cases from among the many capital case appeals made to the Court. In general, the cases selected were those that would give the justices a chance to write a decision that would confirm, change, or add to the existing definition of the "due process" procedures. Their decisions affect how state courts would have to act in capital cases.

Facts About Death Row   The events leading from the death sentence to an appeal in the court of last resort is long, tedious, and costly. In the 1960s, many Death Row inmates got help from lawyers who were members of civil rights organizations like the American Civil Liberties Union and the Legal Defense Fund. Attorneys from the two groups often talked with one another. Funds were raised to pay the costs of arguing appeals in the state and federal court systems. As a result, attorneys representing Death Row inmates began to develop

One method of capital punishment is the firing squad. The prisoner usually sits in a chair, like the one pictured, for execution.

common plans and to share information with each other. Through their cooperation many interesting facts about the use of capital punishment in the United States were found.

They found that almost all the inmates of Death Row were men. Almost all had been convicted of murder or rape. Almost all of them were poor and uneducated. The mental and physical health of these men was strained. Many came close to losing their sanity. Most had been represented in their original trials by court-appointed attorneys who usually lost interest in the case after the first trial. More than half of the persons on Death Row were members of ethnic minorities. In a number of instances, Death Row inmates gave up trying to appeal their sentences. They simply decided they would be better off dead than alive. Such men would reject the attempts of their attorneys to appeal their cases. Instead, they wrote letters to judges and governors requesting immediate execution.

In order to help inmates of Death Row use all the legal options open to them, attorneys from the ACLU and the LDF developed a common strategy. The attorneys began to challenge the death sentences of their clients. They argued in federal courts that their clients' rights to a fair trial—"due process"—had been denied. Often, the attorneys first had to get an order from a governor or a judge delaying, or **"staying,"** the execution of a client. The date might be only a few hours or days away when a "stay" was granted. After the "stay" of execution had been granted, there would be time for the appeals process to run its course until the Supreme Court had agreed or refused to hear the case.

Fairness   When the Supreme Court agreed to hear a case, attorneys then had to write briefs which would show the justices of the Court that due process had been denied. If the original trial of a convicted person had been unfair, the attorney had to prove this. The guilt of the person was not always in dispute. What was in dispute was the fairness or unfairness of the death sentence given to a person for a capital offense.

Defense attorneys asked themselves questions about fairness. How fair was it for rape to be a capital offense in some states but not in others? How fair was it that few educated or rich persons were ever charged with or convicted of a capital offense? How fair was it that prosecution attorneys were able to keep off juries almost every person who said they objected to capital punishment? In such a case, wouldn't the jury that was impartial as to guilt or innocence still be fair in deciding whether the sentence should be life imprisonment or death?

Supreme Court and Capital Punishment   The answers to questions such as these led ACLU and LDF attorneys to argue that discrimination existed. It most frequently resulted in the award of death sentences to Blacks, ethnic minorities, the poor and uneducated. The strongest arguments were based on a study of all the trials that had resulted in a sentence of death for rape. Even though powerful evidence of some discrimination was presented, the Supreme Court never accepted this line of argument.

Attorneys then developed another approach. They argued that all the trials from which jurors who objected to capital punishment had been excluded were unfair. These trials violated the due process requirement.

When the Supreme Court, in 1968, reviewed the case of *Witherspoon v. Illinois* the justices considered the fairness of this method of selecting a jury. Witherspoon was a man convicted of the murder of a Chicago police officer. At his trial, persons stating that they were opposed to capital punishment were excluded from the jury. By 1968, when his appeal reached the Supreme Court, Witherspoon had received a "stay" of execution 15 times. In the *Witherspoon* case the Supreme Court agreed with the reasoning of the defense lawyers that Witherspoon's jury had been unfairly biased in the matter of sentencing.

The nature of the court's decision was such that it applied to all death sentences that had been handed down by a jury from which opponents of the death penalty had been excluded. Hundreds of convicted men's lives were spared by this Supreme Court decision.

After the *Witherspoon* case, ACLU and LDF attorneys hoped they were close to the complete abolition of the death penalty. Most of the men under sentence of death would now get a new look at their sentences. Future capital case juries would contain jurors who would be

Witherspoon (on the right) was a murderer sentenced to death. The Supreme Court ruling in his case affected later death sentences for other prisoners.

willing to argue against a sentence of death. At this point defense attorneys began to think about arguing that the death penalty was now so rare, and that the wait so long as to make the death penalty in the 1970's both "cruel and unusual." It would therefore be forbidden by the Eighth Amendment.

A Landmark Case   On June 28, 1971, the Supreme Court agreed to review four death sentence appeals brought by two rapists (Jackson and Branch) and two murderers (Aikens and Furman). The cases had originated in Texas, California, and Georgia. None of the men qualified for a new trial based on the precedent of *Witherspoon.* There had been no exclusion of jurors who were opposed to capital punishment. Defense attorneys had to argue their cases on grounds that capital punishment itself was "cruel and unusual" and it violated the Eighth Amendment. The lives of almost 100 men still on Death Row around the country depended upon the outcome of the appeal. None of them could hope to appeal their sentences using the Witherspoon ruling.

The three cases were brought together under the heading *Furman* v. *Georgia.* On July 12, 1971, defense lawyers were told when briefs were due. They were informed that the oral argument before the Supreme Court would take place on October 12, 1971. If they expected to win their cases, the defense lawyers had until October 12 to identify arguments that would convince the justices that the sentences of death hanging over the heads of Aiken, Furman, Branch and Jackson, and almost 100 other men were "cruel and unusual." What arguments would do the job?

Defenses of Capital Punishment   In order to do the job, the arguments would have to overcome two major problems. One problem was the argument made by the states. They believed that abolishing executions was the business of state legislatures. The other problem was proving that capital punishment was "cruel and unusual." This was difficult since hardly anybody and certainly not courts had thought of execution for crime as "cruel and unusual" in the first 150 years of the United States. Defense attorneys chose to argue that capital punishment as practiced in the United States in the twentieth century was "cruel and unusual" because it was not fairly applied. Attorneys also said that the Supreme Court should use the power of judicial review to abolish capital punishment rather than wait for the passing of new laws. The basis for these two arguments is found in a set of specific facts.

Objections to Capital Punishment   One fact was that, of the many persons who committed crimes for which execution was a possibility, only a small minority were ever sentenced to death and executed. Some had prosecutors who did not ask for the death penalty. Still others received life imprisonment when found guilty. Some were

granted clemency by the governor of their state. Others successfully appealed on grounds such as *Witherspoon.* In the end, those who were executed seemed to have been chosen almost by lot. No standard was used to select those men or women who were ultimately executed.

Defense attorneys said if a fair standard were applied to the system of capital punishment, many more persons would be executed. The large number of executions would so shock the American public, that there would be a demand for the abolition of capital punishment. Defense attorneys further argued that under the current system of capital punishment, the few people executed would never attract enough attention and concern from state legislatures to cause the abolishment of the death penalty. Often, the brutal nature of the crimes committed by those sentenced to death attracted only demands for their executions. Only in cases where a miscarriage of justice caused the death or near death of an innocent person would legislatures be in favor of proposals to eliminate the death penalty. Therefore, they argued, the Supreme Court should exercise its power of judicial review to declare the death penalty to be "cruel and unusual" punishment and a violation of the Eighth Amendment.

The Supreme Court's ruling in **Furman v. Georgia** did not abolish capital punishment. It said that capital punishment in cases where the jury's right to set a punishment was so unguided. This resulted in the selection of persons to be executed. This was "cruel and unusual" and therefore, forbidden.

Many state legislatures move to restore the possibility of capital punishment. They passed new criminal statutes with built-in sentencing guidelines for capital cases. States also set up two-step capital crimes trials. Under such a procedure, an accused murderer's first trial is held to establish guilt or innocence. A finding of guilty in the first trial leads to a second trial. At this one, a sentence is set. Juries in the second trial can sentence to death only certain people guilty of a capital crime. For instance, murder committed during an armed robbery or while attempting to escape from prison are considered capital offenses worthy of the death penalty. In this second trial the jury cannot sentence to death a guilty person if certain extenuating circumstances were present. If the convicted person had no history of prior criminal activity, or was emotionally disturbed, or acted under the domination of another person, it might not be a capital offense.

When appeals of these new state statutes began to reach the Supreme Court in the late 1970s, certain issues arose and were decided upon. The issues that arose were: Is mandatory execution cruel and unusual? Is execution for a crime in which no life is taken (robbery or rape) cruel and unusual? Are all executions cruel and unusual?

In decisions on a number of appeals including **Gregg v. Georgia** and **Coker v. Georgia**, the Court resolved these issues. Although a number of justices wrote minority, dissenting opinions, all executions are not presently regarded as cruel and unusual. Only mandatory executions of all persons convicted of a certain crime are cruel and unusual. They are forbidden by the Eighth Amendment. Executions for crimes where no life is taken are cruel and unusual and are also forbidden. Death sentences that follow established legal precedents defining the due process procedures—including double trials and sentencing guidelines—which must be available to those found guilty of capital crimes are not cruel and unusual. Such sentences are not forbidden by the Eighth Amendment. In the late 1970s, many state legislatures revised their criminal codes regarding capital crimes to reflect these guidelines.

The Court's Decision   At the close of oral arguments before the court defense attorneys were uncertain of victory. It was not until June 29, 1972 that the court announced its decision. The court found that in the cases before it—Furman, Jackson, Branch, Aikens—capital punishment was unconstitutional because it violated the Eighth and Fourteenth Amendments. Execution in these cases was a violation because no objective standard had been used to decide if these men would be executed. The death sentences of these criminals was "cruel and unusual."

What did the decision mean for the future? Had the death penalty been completely abolished? Since no majority opinion had been written, no specific precedent had been set. The opinions of the five agreeing justices prohibited sentences of death that were made without "objective standards" to guide the sentencing judge or jury. Since the opinion of the court did not add up to an abolition of capital punishment, more capital case appeals were expected to come before the court. No ruling was made on the constitutionality of a state law making execution mandatory for all persons convicted of certain specific crimes such as murder of a police officer or prison guard. Many states either already had or created such laws. Capital punishment still exists, but its administration has been carefully checked by the Supreme Court's decisions in the *Witherspoon* and *Furman* cases.

Gary Gilmore asked for the death sentence in 1977 because he wanted to avoid life imprisonment.

SECTION CHECKUP

1. What constitutional amendments relate to whether executions are legal in the United States?
2. Name four ways a person could escape execution even though found guilty of a capital crime.
3. Why is jury selection so important in a capital case?
4. What two duties do juries have in capital cases?
5. Why does the appeals process last so long in a capital case?
6. Why didn't the *Furman* v. *Georgia* case abolish capital punishment in the United States?
7. What did the Supreme Court find to be unfair about Witherspoon's trial?
8. What did the Supreme Court find to be unfair about Furman's trial?
9. To what power does the term **judicial review** refer?

CHAPTER REVIEW

Sentencing takes place after a person is found guilty of a crime. Punishments serve to deter other crimes, rehabilitate the offender, or both. Jails and prisons are built with deterrence and rehabilitation in mind as well as security. Corrections officials use classification centers to try to match a convicted person's needs with the type of prison where the sentence will be served. Every prison tends to have a high rate of recidivism.

Being imprisoned is not the only form of punishment to which a lawbreaker may be sentenced. Many first offenders are sentenced to probation. Many inmates of prisons serve only part of their sentences before being released on parole. These alternatives are under attack because they fail to deter crime.

The most harsh form of punishment available to society is the taking of a criminal's life. Since 1960, the use of capital punishment in the United States has changed dramatically. Guidelines developed from the opinions of the Supreme Court have cut down the use of capital punishment. It is used only for those heinous crimes where the criminal takes the life of another person. After meeting a strict set of "due process" requirements may a state execute a person convicted of a capital crime. The entire corrections system is designed to meet the needs of society to protect its citizens from the harm that individuals experience when crimes are committed.

QUESTIONS FOR REVIEW

1. Why does society sentence people to prison terms?
2. Why is it important for sentences to be fair?
3. What conditions do persons released on probation or parole generally have to fulfill?
4. How are capital punishment and due process related?
5. What aspects of capital punishment, as it existed in the United States up to 1976, did the Supreme Court find to be "cruel and unusual?"
6. What parts of the corrections system as it now exists in the United States should be retained?

1. Arrange for your class to visit a local jail. Plan carefully to make sure that the visit provides as many as possible of the following experiences:
   a. a briefing for the class by the jail administrator before the tour
   b. thorough tour of the jail by the class members
   c. an opportunity for class members to talk to prisoners
   d. eating prisoner fare in the jail dining facility
   e. explanation of the education and recreation programs available in the jail
   f. interviews with the medical paraprofessionals at the jail. Assistance in arranging such a visit may usually be obtained by contacting the law-related education committee of your local bar association.
2. Simulate a parole board meeting. Select five or seven students to serve as a parole board. Working in groups, write up pre-sentence reports and jail histories of two different prisoners. Each group should then decide privately which prisoner of the two described should be paroled. After individuals on the parole board have studied all the cases, hold a "public hearing" at which the parole board considers and decides all the "cases" brought before it. Conclude the simulation by discussing whether or not the decisions of the parole board were fair. A general discussion of whether or not it is possible to predict the potential behavior of any released prisoner can also be conducted. Are the factors upon which such predictions are based objective or subjective?

YOU AND THE LAW

YOUR LAW LIBRARY

Bedau, Hugo A., ed., *The Death Penalty in America: An Anthology.* Chicago: Aldine, 1964.

Burkhart, Kathryn Watterson, *Women in Prison.* New York: Doubleday, 1973.

Buse, Renee, *The Deadly Silence.* New York: Doubleday, 1965.

Carrington, Frank G., *The Victims.* New York: Arlington, 1975.

Clark, Ramsey, *Crime in America.* New York: Simon and Schuster, 1970.

Harris, Janet, *Crisis In Corrections: The Prison Problem.* New York: McGraw-Hill, 1973.

Harrison, Eddie, *No Time for Dying.* Englewood Cliffs: Prentice-Hall, 1973.

Amendments to the Constitution

(The first ten amendments constitute the Bill of Rights. They became an official part of the Constitution in 1791. They limit the powers of the federal government but not the powers of the states.)

Amendment 1. Freedom of Religion, Speech, Press, Assembly, and Petition (1791)

Congress shall make no law respecting an establishment of religion, or prohibiting the free exercise thereof; or abridging the freedom of speech, or of the press; or the right of the people peaceably to assemble, and to petition the government for a redress of grievances.

Amendment 1. This amendment guarantees to Americans the most essential freedoms. Freedom of religion guarantees the right to worship as one chooses without interference from Congress. The Supreme Court has interpreted this amendment as a guarantee of separation of church and state. Freedoms of speech and press are limited only when they extend to slander and libel (false and malicious statements) or statements that might be injurious to the general welfare of the nation. The First Amendment also entitles the people to hold meetings and to request the government to respond to their grievances.

Amendment 2. Right to Bear Arms (1791)

A well-regulated militia, being necessary to the security of a free state, the right of the people to keep and bear arms shall not be infringed.

Amendment 2. The states have the right to maintain armed militias for their protection. However, the rights of private citizens to own guns can be, and are, regulated by federal and state legislation.

Amendment 3. Housing of Troops (1791)

No soldier shall, in time of peace, be quartered in any house, without the consent of the owner; nor in time of war, but in a manner to be prescribed by law.

Amendment 3. One source of bitter complaint in the colonies had been the British practice of housing their troops in American homes. The Third Amendment guarantees that no soldier will be quartered in a private residence during peacetime, or even in wartime unless under specific congressional legislation.

Amendment 4. Searches and Seizures (1791)

The right of the people to be secure in their persons, houses, papers, and effects, against unreasonable searches and seizures, shall not be violated; and no warrants shall issue but upon probable cause, supported by oath or affirmation, and particularly describing the place to be searched, and the persons or things to be seized.

Amendment 4. This amendment came in response to the British writs of assistance—blanket search warrants permitting officers to search any house at any time. For an American home to be searched, a warrant must be issued by a judge and it must state precisely what the official expects to find.

Amendment 5. Rights of Accused Persons (1791)

No person shall be held to answer for a capital, or otherwise infamous, crime, unless on

Amendment 5. In a federal court no person can be held for a serious crime unless indicted, or charged, by a grand jury. A grand jury is a group of 23 persons who hear in secret the charges against the accused and then decide whether or not the person should be tried in court. "Twice put in

a presentment or indictment of a grand jury, except in cases arising in the land or naval forces, or in the militia, when in actual service in time of war or public danger; nor shall any person be subject for the same offense to be twice put in jeopardy of life and limb; nor shall be compelled, in any criminal case, to be a witness against himself; nor be deprived of life, liberty, or property, without due process of law; nor shall private property be taken for public use, without just compensation.

jeopardy," or double jeopardy, means that no person can be tried twice in federal courts for the same crime.

People cannot be forced to give evidence against themselves that will help prove their guilt. This provision goes back to earlier history when persons were tortured in order to make them confess. This clause allows people on trial to refuse to answer questions when they fear that their answers might convict them of the crime.

"Due process of law" has become quite complicated, but the framers wished to guarantee proper judicial procedures for a person accused of a crime (see Amendment 6). The taking of private property for public use is called the right of "eminent domain." The government cannot take such property without giving owners a fair price for their property. The price is determined by a court.

Amendment 6. Right to a Speedy, Fair Trial (1791)

In all criminal prosecutions, the accused shall enjoy the right to a speedy and public trial, by an impartial jury of the state and district wherein the crime shall have been committed, which district shall have been previously ascertained by law, and to be informed of the nature and cause of the accusation; to be confronted with the witnesses against him; to have compulsory process for obtaining witnesses in his favor, and to have the assistance of counsel for his defense.

Amendment 6. This amendment defines the rights of the accused under due process of law. A person has the right to be informed of the charges against him or her and to a speedy and public trial by jury. Witnesses for and against the accused may be compelled to appear in court to give evidence. The accused is entitled to confront these witnesses and to be represented by an attorney.

Amendment 7. Civil Suits (1791)

In suits at common law, where the value in controversy shall exceed $20, the right of trial by jury shall be preserved, and no fact tried by a jury shall be otherwise reexamined in any court of the United States than according to the rules of the common law.

Amendment 7. If a sum of money larger than $20 is disputed, the people involved may insist on a jury trial. However, in actual practice, cases do not reach federal courts unless much larger sums are involved.

Amendment 8. Bails, Fines, Punishments (1791)

Excessive bail shall not be required, nor excessive fines imposed, nor cruel and unusual punishments inflicted.

Amendment 8. The Eighth Amendment continues an enumeration of the rights of the accused. Before a criminal trial, the accused may be released from jail on payment to the court of a sum of money called bail. Bail is returned if the person comes to trial as ordered. Neither the amount of bail set nor the punishment inflicted should be excessively severe. The Supreme Court has the final say in deciding just what is "excessive," "cruel," and "unusual" in any case.

Amendment 9. Powers Reserved to the People (1791)

The enumeration in the Constitution, of certain rights, shall not be construed to deny or disparage others retained by the people.

Amendment 10. Powers Reserved to the States (1791)

The powers not delegated to the United States by the Constitution, nor prohibited by it to the states, are reserved to the states respectively, or to the people.

Amendment 9. This means that the rights listed in the Constitution are not necessarily the only rights that exist. Other rights shall not be denied to the people, simply because they are not enumerated in the Constitution.

Amendment 10. In the same vein as the previous amendment, the Tenth Amendment stipulates that those powers not extended to the federal government are reserved to the states or the people.

PHOTO CREDITS

Chapter One: pages 2 and 3 UPI; page 6 EPA/Peter Yates; page 7 Burt Glinn/ Magnum; page 8 The Granger Collection, UPI; page 9 The Granger Collection; page 10 Wide World; page 12 Bob Adelman; page 13 Wide World; page 14 UPI; page 18 Michael D. Sullivan; page 21 Patrick A. Burns/New York TIMES.

Chapter Two: page 29 Michael Dobo/EPA; page 33 HRW Photo by Russell Dian; page 35 UPI; page 39 HRW Photo by Alan Mercer; page 43 HRW Photo by Peter Vadnai; page 47 Bob Adelman; page 48 Wide World; page 49 UPI.

Chapter Three: page 51 Bob Adelman, UPI; pages 54 and 55 Brown Brothers; page 58 Laffont/Sygma; page 60 The Granger Collection; page 63 UPI; page 66 Grace/Sygma; page 67 Ginger Chih; page 68 The Bettmann Archive; page 71 Grace/Sygma; page 73 Ginger Chih; page 78 The Bettmann Archive.

Chapter Four: page 85 UPI; page 87 Wide World; page 90 Wide World, UPI; page 92 Bob Adelman; page 93 The Granger Collection; page 97 UPI; page 99 Wide World; page 103 Spring 3100, NYPD; pages 106 and 107 Bob Adelman.

Chapter Five: page 114 UPI; page 117 Wide World; page 119 Michael D. Sullivan; page 121 Peter Karas; page 123 UPI; page 126 Wide World; page 128 Wide World; page 130 UPI; page 133 UPI; page 136 Wide World; page 137 UPI; page 139 Wide World; page 143 UPI.

INDEX